Reading Steps

Robert Hickling / Misato Usukura

KINSEIDO

Kinseido Publishing Co., Ltd.
3-21 Kanda Jimbo-cho, Chiyoda-ku,
Tokyo 101-0051, Japan

Copyright © 2015 by Robert Hickling
　　　　　　　　　Misato Usukura

All rights reserved. No part of this publication may be reproduced, stored in a retrieval system, or transmitted, in any form or by any means, electronic, mechanical, photocopying, recording or otherwise, without the prior permission of the publisher.

First published 2015 by Kinseido Publishing Co., Ltd.

Design: parastyle inc.
Illustrations: Miki Nagai

🎧 音声ファイル無料ダウンロード

https://www.kinsei-do.co.jp/download/3992

この教科書で 🎧 DL 00 の表示がある箇所の音声は、上記 URL または QR コードにて無料でダウンロードできます。自習用音声としてご活用ください。

- ▶ PC からのダウンロードをお勧めします。スマートフォンなどでダウンロードされる場合は、ダウンロード前に「解凍アプリ」をインストールしてください。
- ▶ URL は、検索ボックスではなくアドレスバー（URL 表示覧）に入力してください。
- ▶ お使いのネットワーク環境によっては、ダウンロードできない場合があります。

◎ CD 00　左記の表示がある箇所の音声は、教室用 CD（Class Audio CD）に収録されています。

はしがき

　*Reading Steps*は段階的に学習できるように構成されたリーディング中心の教科書です。この教科書を通して学習することで、基本的な文法事項の確認をし、さらには、より難しいリーディング教材を読みこなすための自信をつけてもらいたいと願っています。

　全24ユニットから成るこの教科書は、各ユニットが5ページで構成されており、2つのリーディングパッセージと簡単な文法説明（練習問題つき）が含まれています。また、各ユニットの最後には、単語力アップのための楽しいタスクが用意されています。

　各ユニットは以下の4つのセクションで構成されています。

Reading Step 1　Getting the Picture

　80〜90語程度の文章を読み、話の流れに合わせて4つのイラストを並べ替えます。文章を読む前あるいはイラストを並べ替えた後に、文章のCDを聞いて内容を確認することができます。（5〜10分）

Reading Step 2　Grammar Made Easy

　このセクションでは文法を勉強します。2ページで構成されており、最初のページではReading Step 1で扱った文章に含まれる文法事項を学習します。簡単な説明と例文を通してポイントを理解した後で、もう一度Reading Step 1の文章を読み直して、学習した文法事項を含んだ個所を探します（"LOOK BACK"）。その後に、選択式と記述式の練習問題が用意されています。

　次のページでは、Reading Step 3に含まれる文法事項を学習します。最初のページと同様に、簡単な説明と例文を通してポイントを理解した後に、2種類の練習問題に取り組みます。いずれも問題によっては音声が収録されていますので、答え合わせなどにご活用ください。（30〜40分）

Reading Step 3　Getting the Idea

　160語〜180語程度の文章を読みながら、空所に入る語句（2択式）を選びます。空所の数は5つなので、無理なく読み進められるでしょう。答えを確認した後で、CDを聞いてあらためて文章の内容を確認します。最後に、文章の内容理解を確認するために、4つの質問（選択式）に答えます。（20〜25分）

Fun with Words

　このセクションでは、クロスワードやワードサーチといった様々な活動を通して、楽しく単語の学習をします。クイズ形式の活動で単語の意味を確認した後に、文を使った空所補充問題などに取り組むことで、文脈の中で単語を使う能力を身につけます。(10～15分)

　最後に、本書作成にあたり、金星堂編集部の皆様から多くのご助言、ご支援をいただきました。この場をお借りして御礼申し上げます。

著者一同

■ 本書は CheckLink（チェックリンク）対応テキストです。

CheckLinkのアイコンが表示されている設問は、CheckLinkに対応しています。
CheckLinkを使用しなくても従来通りの授業ができますが、特色をご理解いただき、授業活性化のためにぜひご活用ください。

CheckLinkの特色について

　大掛かりで複雑な従来のe-learningシステムとは異なり、CheckLinkのシステムは大きな特色として次の3点が挙げられます。
1．これまで行われてきた教科書を使った授業展開に大幅な変化を加えることなく、専門的な知識なしにデジタル学習環境を導入することができる。
2．PC教室やCALL教室といった最新の機器が導入された教室に限定されることなく、普通教室を使用した授業でもデジタル学習環境を導入することができる。
3．授業中での使用に特化し、教師・学習者双方のモチベーション・集中力をアップさせ、授業自体を活性化することができる。

▶教科書を使用した授業に「デジタル学習環境」を導入できる

　本システムでは、学習者は教科書のCheckLinkのアイコンが表示されている設問にPCやスマートフォン、携帯電話端末からインターネットを通して解答します。そして教師は、授業中にリアルタイムで解答結果を把握し、正解率などに応じて有効な解説を行うことができるようになっています。教科書自体は従来と何ら変わりはありません。解答の手段としてCheckLinkを使用しない場合でも、従来通りの教科書として使用して授業を行うことも、もちろん可能です。

▶教室環境を選ばない

　従来の多機能なe-learning教材のように学習者側の画面に多くの機能を持たせることはせず、「解答する」ことに機能を特化しました。PCだけでなく、一部タブレット端末やスマートフォン、携帯電話端末からの解答も可能です。したがって、PC教室やCALL教室といった大掛かりな教室は必要としません。普通教室でもCheckLinkを用いた授業が可能です。教師はPCだけでなく、一部タブレット端末やスマートフォンからも解答結果の確認をすることができます。

▶授業を活性化するための支援システム

　本システムは予習や復習のツールとしてではなく、授業中に活用されることで真価を発揮する仕組みになっています。CheckLinkというデジタル学習環境を通じ、教師と学習者双方が授業中に解答状況などの様々な情報を共有することで、学習者はやる気を持って解答し、教師は解答状況に応じて効果的な解説を行う、という好循環を生み出します。CheckLinkは、普段の授業をより活力のあるものへと変えていきます。

　上記3つの大きな特色以外にも、掲示板などの授業中に活用できる機能を用意しています。従来通りの教科書としても使用はできますが、ぜひCheckLinkの機能をご理解いただき、普段の授業をより活性化されたものにしていくためにご活用ください。

CheckLinkの使い方

CheckLinkは、PCや一部タブレット端末、スマートフォン、携帯電話端末を用いて、この教科書の CheckLink のアイコン表示のある設問に解答するシステムです。
・初めてCheckLinkを使う場合、以下の要領で**「学習者登録」**と**「教科書登録」**を行います。
・一度登録を済ませれば、あとは毎回**「ログイン画面」**から入るだけです。CheckLinkを使う教科書が増えたときだけ、改めて**「教科書登録」**を行ってください。

CheckLink URL
https://checklink.kinsei-do.co.jp/student/

QRコードの読み取りができる端末の場合はこちらから ▶▶▶

ご注意ください! 上記URLは**「検索ボックス」**でなく**「アドレスバー(URL表示欄)」**に入力してください。

▶学習者登録

①上記URLにアクセスすると、右のページが表示されます。学校名を入力し「ログイン画面へ」をクリックしてください。
　PCの場合は「PC用はこちら」をクリックしてPC用ページを表示します。同様に学校名を入力し「ログイン画面へ」をクリックしてください。
②ログイン画面が表示されたら**「初めての方はこちら」**をクリックし「学習者登録画面」に入ります。

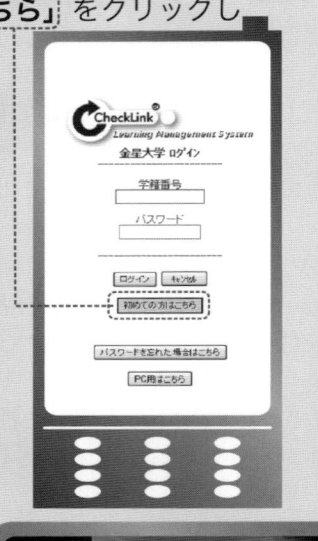
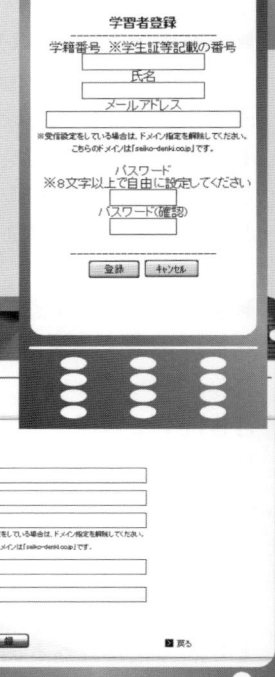

③自分の学籍番号、氏名、メールアドレス(学校のメールなど**PCメールを推奨**)を入力し、次に**任意のパスワード**を8桁以上20桁未満(半角英数字)で入力します。なお、学籍番号はパスワードとして使用することはできません。
④「パスワード確認」は、❸で入力したパスワードと同じものを入力します。
⑤最後に「登録」ボタンをクリックして登録は完了です。次回からは、「ログイン画面」から学籍番号とパスワードを入力してログインしてください。

▶教科書登録

①ログイン後、メニュー画面から「教科書登録」を選び（PCの場合はその後「新規登録」ボタンをクリック）、「教科書登録」画面を開きます。

②教科書と受講する授業を登録します。
教科書の最終ページにある、**教科書固有番号**のシールをはがし、印字された**16桁の数字とアルファベット**を入力します。

③授業を担当される先生から連絡された**11桁の授業ID**を入力します。

④最後に「登録」ボタンをクリックして登録は完了です。

⑤実際に使用する際は「教科書一覧」（PCの場合は「教科書選択画面」）の該当する教科書名をクリックすると、「問題解答」の画面が表示されます。

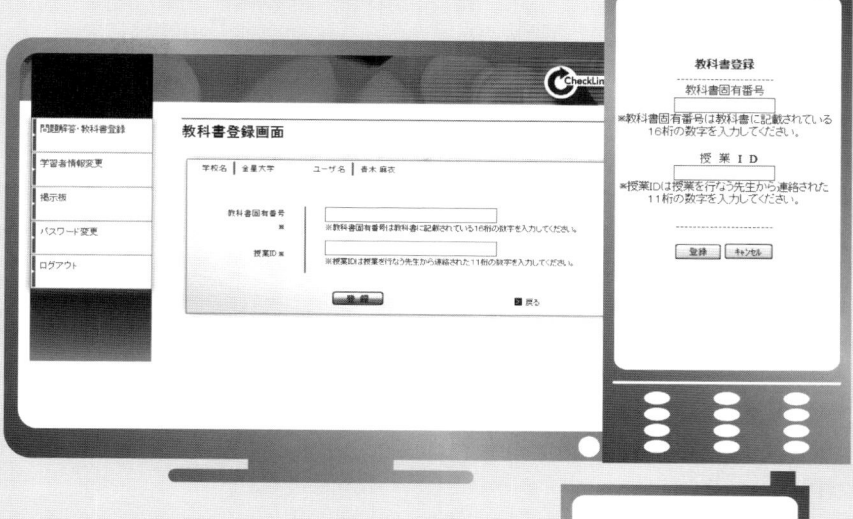

▶問題解答

①問題は教科書を見ながら解答します。この教科書の CheckLink のアイコン表示のある設問に解答できます。

②問題が表示されたら選択肢を選びます。

③表示されている問題に解答した後、「解答」ボタンをクリックすると解答が登録されます。

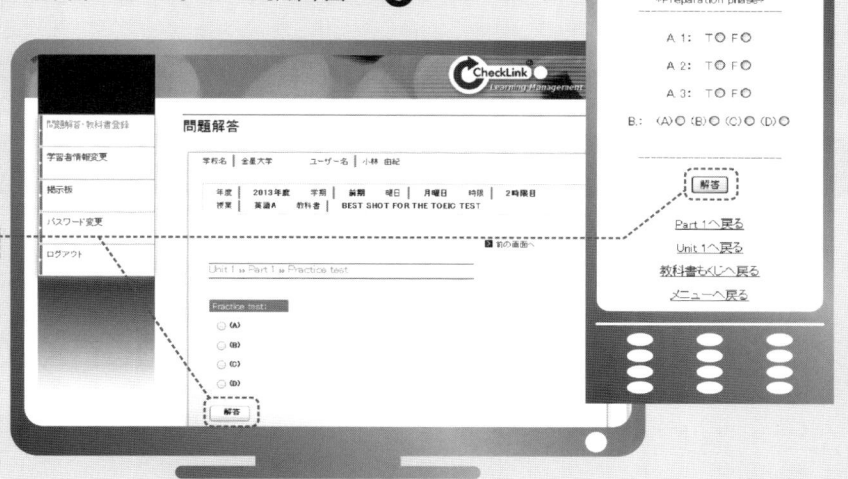

▶CheckLink 推奨環境

PC

推奨 OS
- Windows XP, Vista 以降
- Macintosh OS X 以降
- Linux

推奨ブラウザ
- Internet Explorer 6.0 以上
- Firefox 3.0 以上
- Safari
- Opera
- Google Chrome

携帯電話・スマートフォン
- 3G 以降の携帯電話（docomo, au, softbank）
- iPhone, iPad
- Android OS スマートフォン、タブレット

▶CheckLink 開発

CheckLink は奥田裕司 福岡大学教授、正興 IT ソリューション株式会社、株式会社金星堂によって共同開発されました。

CheckLink は株式会社金星堂の登録商標です。

CheckLink の使い方に関するお問い合わせは…

正興 IT ソリューション株式会社　CheckLink 係

e-mail　checklink@seiko-denki.co.jp

Table of Contents

Unit 1	Marathon Men and Women	be動詞	11
Unit 2	Healthy Choices	命令文	16
Unit 3	Laughing Matters	現在時制	21
Unit 4	Animation the Japanese Way	過去時制	26
Unit 5	Dreams Come True?	現在進行形／過去進行形	31
Unit 6	The Statue of Liberty	Wh疑問文	36
Unit 7	The Taj Mahal and Shah Jahan	可算名詞／不可算名詞	41
Unit 8	Universal Design	代名詞	46
Unit 9	Mars One	will/be going to	51
Unit 10	Getting Around	助動詞	56
Unit 11	The "Meat" of Tomorrow	形容詞	61
Unit 12	Art Crime	副詞	66
Unit 13	Do Animals Know Things We Don't Know?	時を表す前置詞	71
Unit 14	Godiva——The Chocolate and the Lady	場所を表す前置詞	76
Unit 15	Aloha Hawaii	不定詞／動名詞	81
Unit 16	Everyone Loves a Circus	現在完了	86
Unit 17	Text Messaging	too/enough	91
Unit 18	What Type Are You?	句動詞／イディオム	96
Unit 19	Japanese Food Customs	受動態	101
Unit 20	Mascot Characters	5文型	106
Unit 21	Trees——One of Nature's Wonders	比較	111
Unit 22	Koban at Your Service	語句や文をつなぐ接続詞	116
Unit 23	3-D Printers	時や理由などを表す接続詞	121
Unit 24	Fashion Trends Start Here	関係詞節	126

Marathon Men and Women

be動詞

Reading Step 1 Getting the Picture

A 英文を読んで、話の流れに合うように下の絵を並べましょう。

There <u>are</u> many reasons why people run marathons. For most people, the reason is simple—to get fit. Many runners combine this goal with another goal—to help others by running for charity. Another reason for running marathons is to make new friends. Running alone isn't always fun, and most runners are glad to find a training partner. Most marathon runners aren't in it to win. They are in it for the challenge, to do the best they can, and to be able to say, "I did it!"

Notes get fit「健康になる」/ combine A with B「AをBと組み合わせる」/
goal「目標」/ glad「うれしい」/ be in it「参加する」

Reading Step 2　Grammar Made Easy

be 動詞の現在形

「(人・物)は…です」というように、「人・物」(主語)の「状態」や「様子」を説明したい場合は、be 動詞を使います。be 動詞の形は主語に合わせて、以下のように am、are、is と変わります。

I **am** a university student.	私は大学生です。
You **are** beautiful.	あなたは美しいです。
He [She] **is** hungry.	彼 [彼女] はお腹がすいています。
This book [It] **is** very interesting.	この本 [それ] はとてもおもしろいです。
My parents [They] **are** in the garden.	私の両親 [彼ら] は庭にいます。

否定文を作るときは be 動詞の後ろに not をつけます。また、疑問文を作るときは主語の前に be 動詞を置きます。

I **am not** angry anymore.	私はもう怒っていません。
Are you from Osaka?	あなたは大阪の出身ですか。

LOOK BACK もう一度 Reading Step 1 の英文を読んで、be 動詞の現在形に下線を引きましょう。1つ目は1行目の <u>are</u> です。あと6つ見つけられますか。

A （　）内の a〜c から適当な語句を選び、○で囲みましょう。

1. This movie (a. is　b. it's　c. are) really interesting.
2. Brian and I (a. am　b. is　c. are) in the same dance class.
3. Ken and Michelle (a. is a doctor　b. are a doctor　c. are doctors).
4. Are (a. your parents　b. your parents is　c. your parents are) teachers?
5. I (a. am no hungry　b. not hungry　c. am not hungry) now.
6. Our English teacher (a. is America　b. is American　c. are American).

B 空所に適当な be 動詞を入れて、英文を完成させましょう。その後で音声を聞いて答えを確認しましょう。

DL 03　　CD1-03

My name _____ Paulo. I _____ from Brazil. I _____ 19 years old. I have two brothers. Their names _____ Carlos and Marcos. Carlos _____ 17 and Marcos _____ 14. We _____ all soccer fans. _____ you a soccer lover?

12

Marathon Men and Women Unit 1

be動詞の過去形

「(人・物)は…でした」と、主語の過去の「状態」や「様子」を説明したい場合は、be動詞の過去形を使います。現在形と同じように、主語に合わせてwas、wereと形が変わります。

I **was** happy at that time.	あのとき私は幸せでした。
You **were** absent last class.	あなたは前回の授業を欠席しました。
She [He] **was** a famous doctor in the town.	彼女[彼]はその町で有名な医者でした。
The concert [It] **was** fun and exciting.	そのコンサート[それ]はおもしろくてワクワクするものでした。
Bob and Jessica [They] **were** together all the time.	ボブとジェシカ[彼ら]はいつも一緒にいました。

現在形と同じように、否定文を作るときはbe動詞の過去形の後ろにnotをつけます。また、疑問文を作るときは主語の前にbe動詞の過去形を置きます。

You **were not** at the party last night.	あなたは昨夜のパーティーにいませんでした。
Was the test difficult?	そのテストは難しかったですか。

C ( )内のa～dから適当な語句を選び、○で囲みましょう。　CheckLink

1. Kenji (**a.** was　**b.** wasn't　**c.** were　**d.** weren't) at school today. I think he's sick.
2. Brad and his wife (**a.** was　**b.** wasn't　**c.** were　**d.** weren't) classmates in high school, and now they're married.
3. It (**a.** was　**b.** wasn't　**c.** were　**d.** weren't) cold this morning, but now it's warm.
4. We didn't like the restaurant. The food and the service (**a.** was　**b.** wasn't　**c.** were　**d.** weren't) good.
5. (**a.** Was　**b.** Wasn't　**c.** Were　**d.** Weren't) your test easy or difficult?

D 空所に適当なbe動詞の過去形を入れて、会話文を完成させましょう。その後で音声を聞いて答えを確認しましょう。

DL 04　　CD1-04

1. **A:** I love your shoes! _____ they expensive?
   B: No, they _____ expensive. They _____ cheap.
2. **A:** _____ Paris fun?
   B: Yes. The museums _____ excellent, but the weather _____ nice.

13

Reading Step 3 Getting the Idea

A （　）内のa〜bから適当な語句を選び、英文を完成させましょう。その後で音声を聞いて答えを確認しましょう。

In 490 B.C., there was a big battle between the Persians and the Greeks. There ¹(**a.** were **b.** weren't) 48,000 Persian soldiers but only 10,000 Greek soldiers, so the Greeks sent a messenger from Marathon to Sparta to get help. The messenger, Pheidippides, ran for two days. The Spartans told Pheidippides that they would not fight until there ²(**a.** was **b.** wasn't) a full moon.

Pheidippides returned to Marathon with the news. The Greeks ³(**a.** were **b.** weren't) happy. They decided to attack the Persians before help arrived. They won the battle. The Persians ran to their ships and sailed towards Athens to capture the Greek women, children and old people there. Pheidippides' job ⁴(**a.** was **b.** wasn't) finished. He ran to Athens. He told the people of their victory and that the Persians ⁵(**a.** were **b.** weren't) on their way to the city. He then fell to the ground and died.

From this great event, the first marathon race of the modern Olympic Games was run in 1896. A Greek runner, Spiridon Louis, won the race. Like Pheidippides, Spiridon was a kind of postman. It was his job to carry water to Athens.

Notes ▶ B.C.「紀元前」(before Christ「キリスト以前」の略) / the Persians「ペルシャ人」/ the Greeks「ギリシャ人」/ soldier「兵士」/ full moon「満月」/ capture「捕らえる」/ on *one's* way to ...「…へ向かう途中で」

B もう一度英文を読み、1〜4の英文について適切な語句を選びましょう。　CheckLink

1. The story happened about (**a.** 500   **b.** 1,500   **c.** 2,500) years ago.
2. The Greeks attacked the Persians (**a.** with 10,000 soldiers   **b.** when the Spartan soldiers arrived   **c.** before Pheidippides returned).
3. Pheidippides died (**a.** in the battle   **b.** in Athens   **c.** on his way back to Marathon).
4. (**a.** Marathon   **b.** Pheidippides   **c.** Spiridon Louis) won the first marathon race.

Fun with Words ▶ World Geography

A 空所に国や首都、国籍を英語で記入して、表を完成させましょう。

Country	Capital City	Nationality
	Tokyo	Japanese
USA	Washington, D.C.	
		French
England		
	Madrid	
		Thai
Germany		
	Ottawa	
		Egyptian
Russia		Russian

B ( ) 内の a〜d から適当な語句を選び、○で囲みましょう。　CheckLink

1. Mexico is in (**a.** North America   **b.** Central America   **c.** South America).
2. People speak (**a.** Italian   **b.** Portuguese   **c.** Spanish) in Brazil.
3. The Eiffel Tower is in the city of (**a.** London   **b.** Paris   **c.** Barcelona).
4. Greenland is part of (**a.** Canada   **b.** Russia   **c.** Denmark).

Unit 2 Healthy Choices

命令文

Reading Step 1 Getting the Picture

A 英文を読んで、話の流れに合うように下の絵を並べましょう。

CheckLink　DL 06　CD1-06

It is important to replace the water you lose when you sweat. Drinking sports drinks is a good way to supply water, salt and sugar to the body. However, it isn't necessary to buy sports drinks all the time. <u>Try</u> making them yourself. Here's how. Put 1/2 teaspoon of salt and 4 tablespoons of sugar into 1 liter of water. Mix it well. Next, add a slice of lemon. Lemon contains potassium, which is good for your muscles. Cool it before drinking. Cool water lowers your body temperature. Enjoy!

Notes replace「取り替える」/ supply「与える」/ here's …「…は以下の通り」/ potassium「カリウム」/ muscle「筋肉」/ body temperature「体温」

1 ☐ → 2 ☐ → 3 ☐ → 4 ☐

a

b

c

d

Reading Step 2 — Grammar Made Easy

命令文

「…しなさい」と相手に命令したり、「…してください」と指示をしたい場合は、命令文を使います。命令文に主語はなく、動詞から文が始まります。動詞はつねに原形です。

Look at the blackboard.	黒板を見なさい。
Listen to me carefully.	私が言うことを注意深く聞きなさい。
Try again.	もう一度挑戦してみなさい。
Enjoy yourself.	楽しんでね（＝自分自身を楽しみなさい）。
Have a safe trip home.	家まで安全に帰ってね。

命令文にpleaseをつけると、ていねいな口調になります。

Please take care of yourself.	どうぞお大事になさってください。
Have some more cookies**, please**.	どうぞもっとクッキーを召し上がってください。

LOOK BACK もう一度 Reading Step 1の英文を読んで、命令文の動詞に下線を引きましょう。1つ目は3行目の <u>Try</u> です。あと5つ見つけられますか。

A （　）内のa〜cから適当な語句を選び、○で囲みましょう。

1. (a. Drink   b. Drinking   c. To drink) some water. You look hot.
2. (a. You careful   b. Carefully   c. Be careful). The water is very hot.
3. (a. Please hurry   b. Please be hurry   c. You are hurry, please). We're late.
4. (a. Open please the door   b. The door open, please   c. Please open the door).
5. (a. Studies hard   b. Study hard   c. Hard study) for your test.

B 空所に入る動詞を下から選び、会話文を完成させましょう。その後で音声を聞いて答えを確認しましょう。

　　go　have　pass　turn

1. **A:** _____ some more meat and vegetables, Yumi.
   B: Thanks, Mr. Johnson. _____ the potatoes, please.
2. **A:** Excuse me. Is there a train station near here?
   B: Yes. _____ down this street and _____ right at the lights.

否定命令文／命令文の強調

「…してはいけません」という禁止の命令や指示を伝えたい場合は、〈Don't (Do not)＋動詞の原形〉で表します。

| **Don't** take pictures in this room. | この部屋で写真を撮ってはいけません。 |
| **Do not** walk on the grass. | 芝の上を歩いてはいけません。 |

「つねに…しなさい」や「決して…してはいけません」のように、命令文を強調したい場合は、動詞の前にAlwaysやNeverをつけます。Don'tやAlwaysがついても、動詞はつねに原形です。

| **Always** say thank you. | つねにお礼を言いなさい。 |
| **Never** tell a lie. | ウソをついてはいけません。 |

C (　　) 内のa〜cから適当な語句を選び、○で囲みましょう。

1. (**a.** You not forget **b.** Don't forgetting **c.** Don't forget) your textbook.
2. Please (**a.** no talking **b.** don't talk **c.** don't talking) in the library.
3. (**a.** Don't late **b.** Don't be late **c.** Don't you late) for work again!
4. (**a.** Please don't touch **b.** Don't please touch **c.** Don't touch please) it.
5. (**a.** Never there go **b.** Go there never **c.** Never go there). It's not safe.
6. (**a.** Always positive **b.** Always be positive **c.** You always positive).

D 例にならい、(　　) 内の語句を使って、同じ意味の否定命令文になるように書き換えましょう。その後で音声を聞いて答えを確認しましょう。

1. Please stay. ［そこにいてください］
   (go) ⇒ <u>Please don't go</u>.
2. Remember your passport. ［パスポートを忘れないようにしなさい］
   (forget) ⇒ _____.
3. Stay awake. ［起きていなさい］
   (fall asleep) ⇒ _____.
4. Take off your hat, please. ［帽子を脱いでください］
   (wear) ⇒ _____.
5. Stay there. ［そこにいなさい］
   (come here) ⇒ _____.
6. Always keep your promises. ［つねに約束を守りなさい］
   (break) ⇒ _____.

Reading Step 3 — Getting the Idea

A (　)内のa〜bから適当な語句を選び、英文を完成させましょう。その後で音声を聞いて答えを確認しましょう。

The skin is your body's largest organ, and it requires care to stay healthy. Here are some things you can do to take care of your skin.

- Drink plenty of water each day. Water helps to keep your skin from becoming dry and gives it a nice color.
- Eat healthy foods. ¹(**a.** Avoid   **b.** Eat) sugary and oily foods. They are not good for your skin.
- Don't smoke. Smoking can cause wrinkles on the face, rough skin and even skin cancer.
- Always wash your face well with warm water every night before going to bed. ²(**a.** Rinse   **b.** Use) a mild toner and then a moisturizer on your skin after you wash. ³(**a.** Put on   **b.** Take off) any make-up first.
- Never ⁴(**a.** enter   **b.** take) hot showers or baths. Hot water washes away the skin's natural oils. This makes it dry, tight and itchy.
- ⁵(**a.** Put   **b.** Wear) sunscreen all year, even on cloudy days. Sunscreen lets you get sunshine for good health. It also protects you from harmful ultra-violet rays that can cause sunburn and skin cancer.

Notes ▶ organ「器官」／ wrinkle「しわ」／ cancer「がん」／ toner「化粧水」／ moisturizer「保湿剤」／ tight「つっぱった」／ itchy「むずがゆい」

B もう一度英文を読み、1～4の英文について適切な語句を選びましょう。

1. (**a.** Smoking   **b.** Sugary foods   **c.** Cold water) can give you wrinkles.
2. Use a toner and moisturizer on your face (**a.** in the morning   **b.** at night   **c.** each time you wash it).
3. A hot bath makes your skin (**a.** soft   **b.** smooth   **c.** tight).
4. It is a good idea to wear sunscreen (**a.** only on hot summer days   **b.** even on cloudy days   **c.** only on sunny days).

Fun with Words ▶ Health Problems

A 1～8のイラストに合う症状をa～hから選びましょう。

1. (　)　2. (　)　3. (　)　4. (　)

5. (　)　6. (　)　7. (　)　8. (　)

a. cough   **b.** fever   **c.** headache   **d.** sore throat
e. stiff shoulders   **f.** stomachache   **g.** sunburn   **h.** toothache

B 空所に入る適当な語句を **A** から選び、英文を完成させましょう。

1. I have (　　　　　　　) from working at my computer. Can you massage them?
2. I have a bad (　　　　　　　). I think I need to see a dentist.

Laughing Matters

現在時制

Unit 3

Reading Step 1 Getting the Picture

A 英文を読んで、話の流れに合うように下の絵を並べましょう。

 CheckLink　DL 10　CD1-10

We <u>laugh</u> when we feel happy or think something is funny. Some people laugh loudly and use lots of body movements. Others do it quietly and cover their mouth with their hands. Your laughter changes according to the joke and the situation. For example, if you go to a party or a karaoke box with friends, you usually laugh louder and longer. But if you read a funny book on the train or see something funny on your way to school, you usually just smile and laugh quietly to yourself.

Notes　according to ...「…によって、…に従って」

1 ☐ → 2 ☐ → 3 ☐ → 4 ☐

a

b

c

d

Reading Step 2　Grammar Made Easy

一般動詞の現在形

「…が～する」というように、習慣的に行われている動作を表したり、「…は～が好き」というように、心理状態を表したい場合は、be動詞以外の動詞（「一般動詞」といいます）を使います。

I **go** to university by bicycle.	私は大学に自転車で行きます（＝通っています）。
Susan and Amy **like** karaoke very much.	スーザンとエイミーはカラオケが大好きです。

一般動詞の現在形は、次のように形が変化します。

主語（「…は、…が」にあたるもの）がIとyou以外で単数形の場合は、語尾に-sをつける	My father [He] **reads** the newspaper every morning. 私の父［彼］は毎朝、新聞を読みます。
s、sh、ch、o、xで終わる場合は、語尾に-esをつける	Ms. Jones [She] **teaches** us English. ジョーンズ先生［彼女］は私たちに英語を教えています。
子音字＋yで終わ場合は、語尾のyをiに変えて-esをつける	Ben **studies** Japanese history at university. ベンは大学で日本史を勉強しています。

LOOK BACK　もう一度、Reading Step 1の英文を読んで、一般動詞の現在形に下線を引きましょう。1つ目は1行目の<u>laugh</u>です。あと13個見つけられますか。

A　（　）内のa～bから適当な語句を選び、○で囲みましょう。　CheckLink

1. My first class (**a.** start **b.** starts) at 9:00.
2. Nao and Mai (**a.** go **b.** goes) to the same university.
3. Babies (**a.** cry **b.** cries) when they are hungry.
4. Ken's father (**a.** teach **b.** teaches) math.

B　空所に入る動詞を下から選び、英文を完成させましょう（必要に応じて動詞の後ろに-sや-esをつけます）。その後で音声を聞いて答えを確認しましょう。　DL 11　CD1-11

　　do　go　start　work

1. Jim ＿＿＿＿＿ in a bank.
2. We ＿＿＿＿＿ yoga on Sunday mornings.
3. The concert ＿＿＿＿＿ at 7:00.
4. Eri ＿＿＿＿＿ to bed late every night.

一般動詞の現在形の否定文と疑問文

「…は~していない」と一般動詞の現在形の否定文を作るときは、動詞の前にdon'tやdoesn'tをつけます。主語がI、you、複数形の場合はdon'tを、I、you以外の単数形の場合はdoesn'tを使います。動詞はつねに原形のままです。

I **don't like** green peppers.	私はピーマンが好きではありません。
You **don't understand** my idea.	あなたは私のアイデアを理解していません。
Tom **doesn't have** any brothers or sisters.	トムには兄弟も姉妹もいません。

「…は~していますか」と一般動詞の現在形の疑問文を作るときは、文頭にDoやDoesをつけます。主語がI、you、複数形の場合はDoを、I、you以外の単数形の場合はDoesを使い、動詞はつねに原形のままです。

Do you **know** the answer?	その答えを知っていますか。
Does Lisa **walk** to school?	リサは学校まで歩いて通っていますか。
Do they **live** in this apartment?	彼らはこのアパートに住んでいますか。

C （　）内のa～cから適当な語句を選び、○で囲みましょう。

1. Paul (**a.** doesn't eat   **b.** don't eat   **c.** not eat) meat.
2. I'm sorry, I (**a.** not   **b.** am not   **c.** don't) understand your question.
3. Meg and her sister (**a.** doesn't like   **b.** don't like   **c.** doesn't likes) sports.
4. (**a.** Are you live   **b.** Do you live   **c.** Does you live) with your parents?
5. (**a.** Do it   **b.** It does   **c.** Does it) rain a lot in your city?
6. We (**a.** don't has   **b.** doesn't have   **c.** don't have) a television.

D 例にならい、（　）内の語句を並べ替えて、英文を完成させましょう（必要に応じてdoやdoesをつけ加えます）。その後で音声を聞いて答えを確認しましょう。

1. (my computer / not / work)［私のコンピュータは起動しません］
   <u>My computer doesn't work</u>.

2. (I / not / eat / sushi)［私は寿司を食べません］
   _____.

3. (you / like / your university)［あなたはあなたの大学が好きですか］
   _____?

4. (Kenta / have / a part-time job)［健太はアルバイトをしていますか］
   _____?

Reading Step 3 Getting the Idea

A （　）内のa〜bから適当な語句を選び、英文を完成させましょう。その後で音声を聞いて答えを確認しましょう。

　　CheckLink　　DL 13　　CD1-13

　When we laugh we [1](**a.** have　**b.** use) about fifteen muscles in our face. We show our teeth, widen our mouths and narrow our eyes. Sometimes we laugh so hard that we [2](**a.** cry　**b.** sing). Laughing also makes our bodies move. Sometimes our head goes back, our legs lift, our arms wave, and our hands clap together. Everyone around us knows when we are having a good laugh.

　Do you know that laughter is also good for you? Laughter releases a hormone called serotonin into the brain. Doctors often call it the "feel-good" hormone because that's what it does—it makes us feel good. Laughter also helps us to make friends and to be a part of a group. It [3](**a.** gives　**b.** takes) away stress and allows our bodies to work better and feel more relaxed. Laughter [4](**a.** increases　**b.** reduces) pain and helps our bodies fight diseases better, too.

　Laughter is an important part of our lives. It is something that we all share and understand. It doesn't [5](**a.** matter　**b.** care) what language we speak or where we come from. People laugh, on average, about seventeen times a day. How about you? How often do you laugh?

Notes ▶ widen「広げる」/ clap「拍手する」/ release「解放する」/
　　　　　hormone「ホルモン」/ serotonin「セロトニン」/ on average「平均して」

B もう一度英文を読み、1〜4の英文について適切な語句を選びましょう。

1. A person uses about (**a.** 5 **b.** 15 **c.** 50) face muscles to laugh.
2. Serotonin is the name of a (**a.** doctor **b.** medicine **c.** hormone).
3. Laughter helps us to (**a.** interact with people **b.** stay awake **c.** feel pain).
4. The passage says that (**a.** we need to laugh more **b.** laughter is not always good for you **c.** laughing is important in our lives).

Fun with Words ▶ Body Parts

A 身体の一部の名称を書き、クロスワードパズルを完成させましょう。

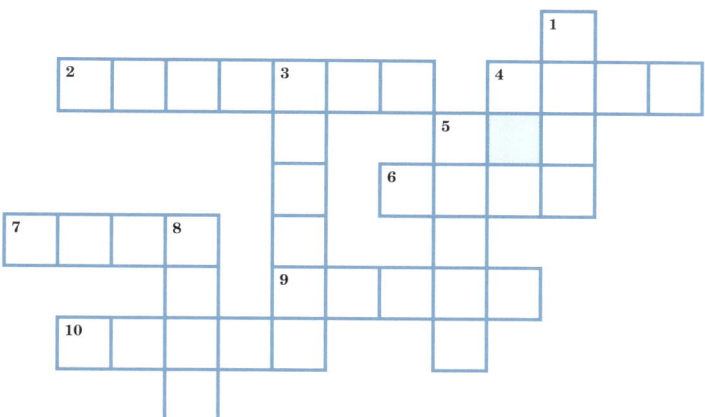

ACROSS
2. We have five of these on each hand.
4. This is between our head and our shoulders.
6. We hear with these.
7. We smell with this.
9. We wear a watch on this.
10. These are in the middle of our legs.

DOWN
1. We need these to walk.
3. These are in the middle of our arms.
5. This is in the middle of our body.
8. We see with these.

B **A**を参考にして、身体の一部を英語で説明してみましょう。その後でペアを組み、おたがいにクイズを出してみましょう。

1. (   ) _____
2. (   ) _____

Unit 4

Animation the Japanese Way

過去時制

Reading Step 1 — Getting the Picture

A 英文を読んで、話の流れに合うように下の絵を並べましょう。

CheckLink　DL 14　CD1-14

Osamu Tezuka was born in 1928 in Osaka.　In third grade he <u>created</u> "Pin Pin Sei-chan," a story with illustrations about a boy with no hair.　Tezuka entered university at the age of 18 and studied to become a doctor.　While in university, he made a comic strip called "Diary of Ma-Chan" ("Maachan no Nikkicho").　He later developed many ideas that we now see in *manga* and *anime*, such as characters with large eyes.　Tezuka died in 1989 at the age of 60.　During his life, he produced more than 700 comics.

Notes　grade「学年」 / while in university「大学在学中に」 /
comic strip「4コママンガ」 / such as ...「…といった」

1 ☐　→　2 ☐　→　3 ☐　→　4 ☐

a

b

c

d

Reading Step 2 — Grammar Made Easy

一般動詞の過去形

「…しました」と過去のことを表現したい場合は、一般動詞の過去形を使います。一般動詞の過去形には、次のように規則変化するものと不規則変化するものがあります。

規則変化するもの	語尾に -ed をつける	Lisa **played** tennis yesterday. リサは昨日テニスをしました。
	e で終わる場合は、語尾に -d だけをつける	We **danced** all through the night. 私たちは一晩中踊りました。
	子音字＋y で終わる場合は、語尾の y を i に変えて -ed をつける	I **studied** for the exam last night. 私は昨夜試験のために勉強しました。
	短母音＋子音字で終わる場合は、語尾の子音字を重ねて -ed をつける	The car **stopped** in front of the bank. その車は銀行の前で止まりました。
不規則変化するもの	go ⇒ went、make ⇒ made、have ⇒ had、take ⇒ took など	My mother **made** a cake for me last weekend. 私の母は先週末、私のためにケーキを作りました。

LOOK BACK もう一度 Reading Step 1 の英文を読んで、過去形の一般動詞に下線を引きましょう。1つ目は1行目の <u>created</u> です。あと6つ見つけられますか。

A （　）内の a〜c から適当な語句を選び、○で囲みましょう。　　CheckLink

1. Alex (a. sale   b. sell   c. sold) his car for $1,000.
2. We really (a. were enjoy   b. did enjoyed   c. enjoyed) today's class.
3. Sam (a. choice   b. chose   c. choose) to study Japanese at university.
4. I stayed home last night and (a. watched   b. did watched   c. was watched) an old movie on TV.
5. Hanae (a. sang   b. song   c. sung) a song in English at the karaoke box.

B （　）内の語句を使って、会話文を完成させましょう（必要に応じて動詞を過去形に変えます）。その後で音声を聞いて答えを確認しましょう。

DL 15　CD1-15

A: _____ bowling yesterday. (Jim and I / go)
B: I thought _____ baseball practice. (you / have)
A: Well, the weather was bad, so the coach _____. (cancel / it)

一般動詞の過去形の否定文と疑問文

「…は〜しませんでした」と一般動詞の過去形の否定文を作るときは、動詞の前にdidn'tをつけます。動詞はつねに原形のままです。

| **We didn't** watch TV last night. | 私たちは昨夜テレビを見ませんでした。 |

「…は〜しましたか」と一般動詞の過去形の疑問文を作るときは、文頭にDidをつけます。動詞はつねに原形のままです。

| **Did** you go to the party with Mary?
— Yes, I **did**.
— No, I **didn't**. | あなたはメアリーと一緒にパーティーに行きましたか。
— はい、行きました。
— いいえ、行きませんでした。 |

C (　) 内のa〜cから適当な語句を選び、○で囲みましょう。

1. I (a. not have   b. didn't have   c. didn't had) time to eat lunch today.
2. Did you (a. finish your homework   b. your homework finish   c. finished your homework)?
3. Arisa liked the movie, but (a. I'm not liked   b. I didn't   c. I wasn't).
4. (a. Did you sleep   b. Were you slept   c. Were you sleep) well last night?
5. I really (a. didn't want   b. not wanted   c. didn't wanted) to go there.
6. I saw Moe, but I (a. saw   b. didn't saw   c. didn't see) Rie.

D (　) 内の語句を使って、会話文を完成させましょう（必要に応じて語句を加えたり、動詞を過去形に変えます）。その後で音声を聞いて答えを確認しましょう。
　DL 16　　CD1-16

1. A: Mike, _____ the cookies on the counter? (you / eat)
   B: Yes, _____. And they were delicious! (I / do)
   A: _____ them for you. (I / not / make)
   _____ them for my boyfriend. (I / bake)
   B: Oh, sorry.

2. A: _____ soccer yesterday, Frank? (you / play)
   B: Yes, _____. (I / do)
   A: _____ the game? (you / win)
   B: No, _____. (we / not / win) _____.
   (we / lose)

Reading Step 3 Getting the Idea

A ( )内のa～bから適当な語句を選び、英文を完成させましょう。その後で音声を聞いて答えを確認しましょう。

CheckLink   DL 17   CD1-17

Japanese people first saw Osamu Tezuka's *Astro Boy* ("Tetsuwan Atomu") in 1963. It was Japan's first animation television series. It quickly became popular, and the demand for more weekly TV animation programs in Japan ¹(**a.** increased   **b.** decreased). This was a problem, however. Until then Japanese animators followed the Disney style of animation. They used many cels to create realistic movements. Japanese animators ²(**a.** had   **b.** didn't have) the time or money to do this, so they made fewer cels. This resulted in fewer movements.

Because there were fewer cels, animators ³(**a.** looked   **b.** paid) for new ways to make their stories look more interesting. They studied the techniques of American animators. They ⁴(**a.** knew   **b.** learned) that American animators usually used the same angle for each scene. Japanese animators began drawing scenes from different angles. They also thought of the idea of using backgrounds based on real life locations. Later, one production company started drawing important shots with more detail than the rest of the work. This became known as "money shot" animation. These ideas ⁵(**a.** helped   **b.** didn't help) to make Japanese *anime* unique and world famous.

Notes cel「(アニメーションの) セル画」(celluloid pictureの略) / angle「角度」/ based on ...「…に基づいて」/ detail「細部」

B もう一度英文を読み、1〜4の英文について適切な語句を選びましょう。

1. Japan's first animation television series was called (a. *Iron Man*   b. *Atomic Boy*   c. *Astro Boy*) in English.
2. Japanese animators cut the number of cels to (a. save time and money   b. make shorter stories   c. have fewer movements).
3. American animators used (a. one scene for each story   b. the same angle for each scene   c. real life locations as backgrounds).
4. "Money shot" animation means (a. making all the characters the same size   b. using no backgrounds   c. using more detail to animate important scenes).

Fun with Words ▶ Jobs

A 例にならい、空所に職業を表す単語を入れてみましょう。最初の1文字目はあたえられています。

1. I bake bread. I am a b<u>aker</u>.
2. I play the piano. I am a p_____.
3. I serve people in a restaurant. I am a w_____.
4. I act in movies. I am a movie a_____.
5. I play music. I am a m_____.
6. I make sick people well. I am a d_____.
7. I teach at a university. I am a p_____.
8. I do magic. I am a m_____.
9. I fix people's teeth. I am a d_____.
10. I work in a library. I am a l_____.

B **A**を参考にして、例文を2つ作ってみましょう。

1. I _____. I am a _____.
2. I _____. I am a _____.

Dreams Come True?

現在進行形／過去進行形

Unit 5

Reading Step 1 Getting the Picture

A 英文を読んで、話の流れに合うように下の絵を並べましょう。

What do your dreams mean? Here is what some experts think.
- You <u>are flying</u>. → Perhaps people see you as a leader.
- You are outside, but you are wearing your pajamas, or you aren't wearing anything at all. → Maybe your brain is trying to help you escape a difficult situation.
- You are taking a test that you didn't study for. → Perhaps your dream is telling you to study harder.
- You are dreaming about an alien. → This might help you when you are feeling nervous about starting something new.

Notes　expert「専門家」／ escape「逃げる」／ nervous「神経質な」

1 ☐ → 2 ☐ → 3 ☐ → 4 ☐

Reading Step 2 Grammar Made Easy

現在進行形

「今…しています」と、現在進行中の動作を表現したい場合は、現在進行形を使います。現在進行形は、〈be 動詞の現在形 ＋ 一般動詞の ing 形〉で表します。

| I **am doing** my homework now. | 私は今、宿題をしています。 |
| Miho **is baking** cookies in the kitchen. | ミホはキッチンでクッキーを焼いています。 |

現在進行形の否定文を作るときは、be 動詞の後ろに not をつけます。また、疑問文を作るときは、主語の前に be 動詞を置きます。

| I'm **not feeling** well. | 私は気分が悪いです（よい気分がしていません）。 |
| **Are** you **waiting** for Ken? | あなたはケンを待っているのですか。 |

LOOK BACK もう一度 Reading Step 1 の英文を読んで、現在進行形に下線を引きましょう。1つ目は 2 行目の <u>are flying</u> です。あと 7 つ見つけられますか。

A （　）内の a 〜 c から適当な語句を選び、○で囲みましょう。

1. Ken and Michelle (**a.** have   **b.** is having   **c.** are having) lunch now.
2. Laura (**a.** isn't study   **b.** not studying   **c.** isn't studying). She's sleeping.
3. (**a.** Is the baby sleeping   **b.** The baby it's sleeping   **c.** Is sleeping the baby)?
4. I think everyone (**a.** having   **b.** is having   **c.** are having) a good time.
5. Mr. and Mrs. Jones (**a.** isn't   **b.** aren't   **c.** they aren't) wearing coats. They look cold.
6. Peter's (**a.** baking cookies   **b.** cookies baking   **c.** is baking cookies).

B 例にならい、（　）内の語句を使って、現在進行形の英文を完成させましょう。その後で音声を聞いて答えを確認しましょう。

1. (Goro / take) ⇒ <u>Is Goro taking</u> a shower?
2. (Aki / sit) ⇒ _____ on the bench.
3. (you / enjoy) ⇒ _____ the party?
4. (It / not / rain) ⇒ _____ today.

過去進行形

「あのとき…していました」と、過去のある時点で進行中だったことを表現したい場合は、過去進行形を使います。過去進行形は、〈be動詞の過去形+一般動詞のing形〉で表します。

| I **was playing** basketball in the gym then. | そのとき私は体育館でバスケットボールをしていました。 |

過去進行形の否定文を作るときは、be動詞の後ろにnotをつけます。また、疑問文を作るときは、主語の前にbe動詞を置きます。

| We **were not watching** TV at that time. | あのとき私たちはテレビを見ていませんでした。 |
| **Was** she **working** at her office around 9:00 last night**?** | 昨夜9時ごろ、彼女は会社で働いていましたか。 |

C （　）内のa～cから適当な語句を選び、○で囲みましょう。

1. A lot of people (a. waiting   b. was waiting   c. were waiting) to buy tickets.
2. Were (a. you   b. your   c. you're) living in Australia last year?
3. At 6:00 (a. it was shining the sun   b. the sun shining   c. the sun was shining).
4. It (a. wasn't snowing   b. wasn't snow   c. weren't snowing) earlier, but it is now.
5. (a. Were the player practicing   b. Was the player practicing   c. Was practicing the player) in the rain?
6. No one (a. was listening   b. were listening   c. wasn't listening) to the speech.

D 例にならい、（　）内の語句を使って、過去進行形の英文を完成させましょう。その後で音声を聞いて答えを確認しましょう。

1. (I / live / in London) ⇒ <u>I was living in London</u> at that time.
2. (you / write / your report)
   ⇒ _____ in the library?
3. (they / eat / pizza / and / drink / cola)
   ⇒ _____.
4. (Greg / not / talk / to anyone)
   ⇒ _____. He was angry.

Reading Step 3 Getting the Idea

A (　) 内のa〜bから適当な語句を選び、英文を完成させましょう。その後で音声を聞いて答えを確認しましょう。

CheckLink　DL 21　CD1-21

　The American Elias Howe invented the sewing machine in 1845. He had the idea of a machine with a needle going through a piece of cloth. The problem was that he didn't know how to build it … until he had a dream. In his dream, Howe was ¹(**a.** eating　**b.** running away from) cannibals in Africa. The cannibals caught him. They told him that they would eat him if he didn't build his machine by the next morning. Howe couldn't do it.

　The next day, the cannibals were ²(**a.** cooking　**b.** playing with) him in a large pot. They were ³(**a.** burning　**b.** dancing) around the fire and moving their spears up and down. Howe saw a small hole at the end of the spears. When he woke up from his dream, Howe remembered the up-and-down motion of the spears and the position of the holes. Soon he was ⁴(**a.** drilling　**b.** sewing) a small hole near the pointed end of a needle, and ⁵(**a.** watching　**b.** pushing) it through a piece of cloth. Howe's idea worked, thanks to a dream about trying to build a sewing machine for cannibals in a faraway country.

Notes Elias Howe「エリアス・ハウ」(アメリカの発明家。1819–1867) / invent「発明する」/ sewing machine「ミシン」/ needle「針」/ cloth「布」/ cannibal「人食い人種」/ spear「やり」/ pointed「先のとがった」/ work「うまくいく」/ faraway「遠くの」

B もう一度英文を読み、1〜4の英文について適切な語句を選びましょう。

1. (**a.** An African man **b.** A man from the United States **c.** Some African cannibals) invented the sewing machine.
2. In Howe's dream (**a.** cannibals ate him **b.** he was not able to build a sewing machine **c.** he invented the sewing machine).
3. The cannibals made holes in their (**a.** noses **b.** ears **c.** spears).
4. When Howe woke up, he (**a.** drilled a hole in a needle **b.** jumped up and down **c.** did not remember his dream).

Fun with Words ▶ Great Inventions

A 例にならい、それぞれの日本語に合う英語の語句を見つけてみましょう。語句は上下左右に読めるものとします。

```
Q H C C O M P U T E R T
B Y M O V A R P E Y T E
L X P L Z H K H L G E L
U U G F U D J C E F N E
B C A M E R A X V P R P
T A U T O M O B I L E H
H G Z Q H S L I S B T O
G U E N A L P R I A N N
I I T T O Q U V O T I E
L B A O P D M X N M B Q
```

1. 飛行機　__ __ __ __ __ __ __ __
2. 自動車　__ __ __ __ __ __ __ __ __ __
3. カメラ　__ __ __ __ __ __
4. コンピュータ　*COMPUTER*
5. インターネット　__ __ __ __ __ __ __ __
6. 電球　__ __ __ __ __ __ __ __ __
7. 電話　__ __ __ __ __ __ __ __ __
8. テレビ　__ __ __ __ __ __ __ __ __ __

B 空所に入る適当な語句を**A**から選び、英文を完成させましょう。

1. The fastest way to travel between Tokyo and New York is by (　　　　　).
2. Thomas Elva Edison invented the (　　　　　).
3. Let me take your picture with my cell phone (　　　　　).

Unit 6

The Statue of Liberty

Wh 疑問文

Reading Step 1 — Getting the Picture

A 英文を読んで、話の流れに合うように下の絵を並べましょう。

CheckLink　DL 22　CD1-22

The Statue of Liberty is the world's most famous statue. Here are some common questions about it. Do you know the answers?
- Where is the statue?　• Who designed it?　• When was it built?
- What is it made of?　• Why is it green?

The Statue of Liberty is on Liberty Island in New York. The statue was designed by a Frenchman named Frédéric-Auguste Bartholdi and built in the late 1800s. It's made of copper. However, the oxygen in the air changed its copper color to green.

Notes ▶ Statue of Liberty「自由の女神」/ Frédéric-Auguste Bartholdi「フレデリック・オーギュスト・バルトルディ」(フランスの彫刻家。1834–1904) / copper「銅」/ oxygen「酸素」

1 ☐ → 2 ☐ → 3 ☐ → 4 ☐

36

Reading Step 2　Grammar Made Easy

Whではじまる疑問文

「誰が」「何を」などの情報をたずねたい場合は、疑問詞を使って疑問文を作ります。

ルール1	疑問詞（＝たずねたい情報）は疑問文の文頭に置きます。
ルール2	疑問詞の後には、be動詞を使った疑問文や、do、does、didを使った疑問文が続きます。ただし、「誰が…しますか（しましたか）」（下記②参照）、「何が…しますか（しましたか）」（下記④参照）という意味の疑問文のときは、疑問詞の後にすぐ動詞が続きます。

①	**Who** do you like best among the four?	その4人の中であなたは誰を一番好きですか。
②	**Who** sent this letter to you?	誰があなたにこの手紙を送ったのですか。
③	**What** did he buy for her birthday?	彼は彼女の誕生日に何を買いましたか。
④	**What** made you angry?	何があなたを怒らせたのですか。
⑤	**Where** did you go last weekend?	先週末、あなたはどこへ行きましたか。
⑥	**When** is your birthday?	あなたの誕生日はいつですか。
⑦	**Why** does she want to go there?	なぜ彼女はそこへ行きたがっているのですか。

LOOK BACK　もう一度 Reading Step 1の英文を読んで、本文に書かれている5つの質問の答えに当たる部分に下線を引きましょう。最初の質問の答えは <u>on Liberty Island in New York</u> です。残りの4つの質問についても同様に答えを探してみましょう。

A　(　)内のa〜cから適当な語句を選び、○で囲みましょう。

1. Who (a. live　b. does live　c. lives) in that house?
2. (a. What　b. Why　c. Who) is Jim late?
3. Where (a. are you go　b. you went　c. did you go) last night?
4. When (a. starts the lesson　b. does the lesson start　c. is the lesson start)?
5. What (a. does this word mean　b. does mean this word　c. means this word)?

B　例にならい、太字部分が答えになるような疑問文を作りましょう。その後で音声を聞いて答えを確認しましょう。

1. She's **my aunt**.　⇒　<u>Who</u> is she?
2. The game is **today**.　⇒　_____ is the game?
3. He will go to **L.A.**　⇒　_____ will he go?

How を使った疑問文

疑問詞の How を使うと、いろいろな意味の疑問文を作ることができます。

How ...? 「どのように…？」	**How** do you go to school? — I go to school by bus.	あなたはどのように学校に通っていますか。 — 私はバスで学校に通っています。
How much/many ...? 「どのくらいたくさん（の）…？」	**How much** are these shoes? — They are 5,000 yen.	この靴はいくらですか。 — 5,000 円です。
	How many comic books does he have? — He has more than 300 comic books.	どのくらいたくさんの（何冊の）マンガを彼は持っていますか。 — 彼は 300 冊以上のマンガを持っています。
How＋形容詞/副詞 ...? 「どのくらい…？」	**How tall** is the Tokyo Skytree? — It's 634 meters tall.	東京スカイツリーはどのくらい高いですか。 — 634 メートルです。
	How fast can he run? — He can run 100 meters in 11 seconds.	彼はどのくらい速く走ることができますか。 — 彼は 100 メートルを 11 秒で走ることができます。

C （　）内の a〜c から適当な語句を選び、○で囲みましょう。　　CheckLink

1. (a. How tall   b. How high   c. How centimeters) are you? — I'm 165 cm.
2. (a. How   b. How many   c. How much) time do we have? — Two hours.
3. How (a. big   b. size   c. wide) is your apartment? — It's 45 m^2.
4. How (a. long   b. time   c. long time) did it take you to get here? — An hour.

D 空所に入る適当な語句を下から選び、疑問文を完成させましょう。その後で音声を聞いて答えを確認しましょう。

DL 24　CD1-24

　　　cold　far　high　much

1. How _____ do you weigh, Tim? — 60 kilograms.
2. How _____ is Mount Everest? — It's almost 9,000 meters.
3. How _____ is it from your house to the station? — It's about one kilometer.
4. How _____ does it get in your hometown in winter? — Sometimes it's −40°C.

Reading Step 3 — Getting the Idea

A ( )内のa～bから適当な語句を選び、英文を完成させましょう。その後で音声を聞いて答えを確認しましょう。

CheckLink　DL 25　CD1-25

The Statue of Liberty was a gift from France to the United States. The French planned to give the statue to the U.S. on July 4, 1876 to celebrate America's 100th birthday. However, the United States didn't receive its gift until 1886.

- 1(a. When　b. Why) did the gift arrive late? France built the statue, and America built the base for it. Both sides had trouble raising money though, so it took longer to finish.
- 2(a. How wide　b. How tall) is the statue? It's around 100 meters from the ground to the top of the torch. The statue itself is about half that height.
- 3(a. How much　b. How many) does it weigh? The statue is about 200,000 kilograms, or the weight of about 35 elephants.
- 4(a. Why　b. How) did the statue get from France to the U.S.? To prepare for the journey by ship across the Atlantic Ocean, the statue was taken apart and its 350 pieces were packed into 214 crates.
- 5(a. What　b. How many) people come to see the statue each year? Each year around four million people visit the Statue of Liberty, or about 10,000 a day.

Notes celebrate「祝福する」/ raise money「資金を集める」/ torch「たいまつ」/ height「高さ」/ weigh「重さがある」/ take apart「分解する」/ crate「木箱」

B もう一度英文を読み、1〜4の英文について適切な語句を選びましょう。　　CheckLink

1. France gave the Statue of Liberty to the United States in (**a.** 1776　**b.** 1876　**c.** 1886).
2. The statue without the base is about (**a.** 50　**b.** 100　**c.** 200) meters tall.
3. The statue was (**a.** cut into 214 pieces　**b.** put into wooden boxes　**c.** packed into 350 crates) and then shipped to New York.
4. The Statue of Liberty receives about (**a.** 400,000　**b.** 4,000,000　**c.** 40,000,000) visitors a year.

Fun with Words ▶ Numbers

A あたえられた数字の連続を参考にして、空所に入る数字を英語で書いてみましょう。

1. two, four, six, eight, ten, _____, _____, _____
2. one, two, four, seven, eleven, _____, _____
3. one, four, nine, sixteen, twenty-five, _____, _____
4. one, ten, one hundred, one thousand, _____, _____

B 次の数字を英語で書いてみましょう。

1. 1　_____
2. 12　_____
3. 123　_____
4. 1,234　_____
5. 12,345　_____
6. 123,456　_____

C 次の文を読み、空所に入る数字を英語で書いてみましょう。

Emi makes nine hundred fifty yen an hour. She worked for six hours on Saturday and eight hours on Sunday. How much money did Emi earn on the weekend?

Answer: _____ yen

The Taj Mahal and Shah Jahan

Unit 7

可算名詞／不可算名詞

Reading Step 1 Getting the Picture

A 英文を読んで、話の流れに合うように下の絵を並べましょう。

CheckLink　DL 26　CD1-26

The Taj Mahal is a mausoleum in India and one of the most beautiful structures in the world. Shah Jahan was a king in the early 17th century. He built the Taj Mahal as a resting place for the last of his three wives, Mumtaz Mahal. She died when she gave birth to their fourteenth child. There are four pillars around the main dome. Two red sandstone buildings stand beside the main mausoleum. Beautiful gardens surround the Taj Mahal. There is also a large reflecting pool which doubles its beauty.

Notes　the Taj Mahal「タージ・マハル」 / mausoleum「墓、霊廟（れいびょう）」 / structure「建造物」 / pillar「柱、尖塔」 / sandstone「砂岩」 / reflecting「反射する」 / pool「水たまり」

1 ☐ → 2 ☐ → 3 ☐ → 4 ☐

a

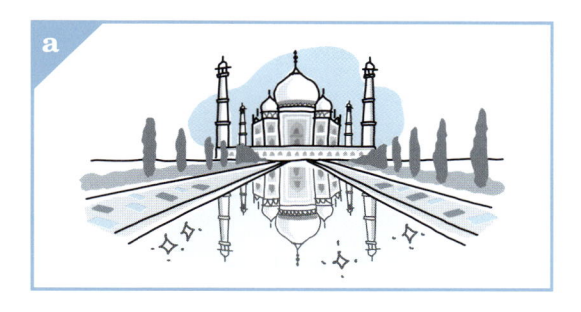

b

c

d

Reading Step 2: Grammar Made Easy

数えられる名詞の複数形

英語の名詞には、bookのように数えられるものと、waterのように数えられないものがあります。数えられる名詞の複数形を作りたい場合は、下の表のように名詞の後ろに-sなどをつけます。

語尾に-sをつける	book – book**s** / picture – picture**s**
語尾に-esをつける (s、ss、sh、ch、o、xで終わる場合)	bus – bus**es** / peach – peach**es** / tomato – tomato**es**
語尾を変えて-s/-esをつける (子音字＋y、f、feで終わる場合)	country – countr**ies** / knife – kni**ves**
不規則変化するもの	man – **men** / woman – **women** / mouse – **mice** / foot – **feet**

＊数えられる名詞の中には、people「人々」、family「家族」、fish「魚の群れ」、sheep「羊の群れ」など、集合体を表しているために、-sがつかなくても複数扱いされるものがあります。

LOOK BACK もう一度、Reading Step 1の英文を読んで、名詞の複数形に下線を引きましょう。1つ目は1行目の <u>structures</u> です。あと4つ見つけられますか。

A （ ）内のa～bから適当な語句を選び、○で囲みましょう。　CheckLink

1. There are many beautiful (**a.** garden　**b.** gardens) in Kyoto.
2. Are the (**a.** child　**b.** children) playing outside?
3. I bought a table and two (**a.** chair　**b.** chairs) for my new apartment.
4. This (**a.** watermelon　**b.** watermelons) is delicious.
5. Could you tell me your telephone (**a.** number　**b.** numbers)?
6. It's a beautiful day. There are no (**a.** cloud　**b.** clouds) in the sky.

B （　）内の語句を必要に応じて複数形に変えて、会話文を完成させましょう。その後で音声を聞いて答えを確認しましょう。　DL 27　CD1-27

A: I think the ＿＿＿＿＿＿＿ (salad) needs more ＿＿＿＿＿＿＿＿＿＿ (vegetable). Let's buy a ＿＿＿＿＿＿＿＿＿ (cucumber) and some ＿＿＿＿＿＿＿ (tomato) to put in it.

B: OK. And let's get some ＿＿＿＿＿＿＿＿＿ (mushroom) and an ＿＿＿＿＿＿＿ (avocado), too.

数えられない名詞

数えられない名詞は通常は複数形にはしません。「たくさんの…」「1杯の…」のように、数量を表したい場合は、修飾語句をつけます。

抽象名詞	形のないものや抽象的な概念を表す名詞	love「愛情」、friendship「友情」、creation「創造」、beauty「美しさ」 All we need is **love**. 私たちに必要なのは愛情です。
集合名詞	ひとまとまりの集合体を表す名詞	furniture「家具」、baggage「手荷物」、machinery「機械類」 John bought **furniture** for his new office. ジョンは新しいオフィス用の家具を買いました。
物質名詞	液体、気体、原料、食料などを表す名詞	water「水」、sugar「砂糖」、paper「紙」、wood「木」、bread「パン」、cheese「チーズ」 Please give me a glass of **water**. 私に1杯の水をください。

C （　）内のa〜cから適当な語句を選び、○で囲みましょう。

1. Anne has (a. red hair　b. a red hair　c. red hairs).
2. Would you like (a. a milk　b. some milk　c. some milks) for your coffee?
3. Yumiko is a vegetarian. She doesn't eat (a. meat　b. meats　c. a meat).
4. Look at all (a. a snow　b. snows　c. the snow) on the ground!
5. I haven't got (a. time　b. a time　c. times) to do my homework.
6. How many (a. piece of cakes　b. pieces of cake　c. pieces of cakes) did you eat?

D （　）内の語句を必要に応じて複数形に変えて、会話文を完成させましょう。その後で音声を聞いて答えを確認しましょう。

　　　　　　　　　　　　　　　　　　　　　　　　　　DL 28　　CD1-28

1. **A:** Did you eat breakfast?

   B: Yes. I had two ＿＿＿＿＿ of toast and a ＿＿＿＿ of coffee. (slice / cup)

2. **A:** I love your ＿＿＿＿＿＿. What kind of ＿＿＿＿ is it made of?

   　　　　　　　　　　　　　　　　　　　　　　　　　(furniture / wood)

   B: It's oak.

Reading Step 3 — Getting the Idea

A （　）内のa〜bから適当な語句を選び、英文を完成させましょう。その後で音声を聞いて答えを確認しましょう。

The Mughal Empire controlled most of India and Pakistan in the 16th and 17th ¹(**a.** century **b.** centuries). Shah Jahan became king in 1627, at the age of 35. While he was king, he successfully expanded the empire to the south.

Shah Jahan was also the most creative builder in the history of India. He is most famous for his creation of the Taj Mahal. He also built the Jama Masjid in Delhi, which is the largest mosque in India. He added several styles of his own, including the use of ²(**a.** marble **b.** marbles).

In 1657, Shah Jahan's third son Aurangzeb became king. This, however, was not until after a violent fight for ³(**a.** power **b.** powers). In that fight he killed his two brothers and put his father in prison. Aurangzeb kept his father in Agra Fort, where he would spend the rest of his ⁴(**a.** day **b.** days). From Agra Fort, Shah Jahan could see the Taj Mahal across the Yamuna River. After his death in 1666, Shah Jahan was placed beside his wife inside the Taj Mahal. To this day, the Taj Mahal remains a symbol of eternal ⁵(**a.** love **b.** loves).

Notes Mughal Empire「ムガル帝国」/ Jama Masjid「ジャーマー・マスジド」/ mosque「モスク、イスラム教寺院」/ marble「大理石」/ put ... in prison「…を投獄する」/ Agra Fort「アーグラ城塞」/ Yamuna River「ヤムナー川」/ eternal「永遠の」

B もう一度英文を読み、1〜4の英文について適切な語句を選びましょう。

1. Shah Jahan became king of the Mughal Empire in the (**a.** 15th **b.** 16th **c.** 17th) century.
2. Jama Masjid is (**a.** a city in India **b.** a mosque in Delhi **c.** the name of Shah Jahan's wife).
3. Aurangzeb was Shah Jahan's (**a.** brother **b.** father **c.** son).
4. Shah Jahan died in (**a.** Agra Fort **b.** the Taj Mahal **c.** the Yamuna River).

Fun with Words ▶ One Piece, Two Pieces...

A 次の名詞の複数形を書いてみましょう。

1. baby — babies
2. boy —
3. chair —
4. child —
5. class —
6. dish —
7. family —
8. foot —
9. leaf —
10. man —
11. party —
12. peach —
13. person —
14. potato —
15. sheep —
16. shoe —
17. tooth —
18. wife —
19. woman —
20. zoo —

B ( )内の文字を並べ替えて、会話文を完成させましょう。最初の1文字目はあたえられています。

A: I don't like green peas. Are there any v _ _ _ _ _ _ _ _ _ that you don't like? (g e t a v b l e e s)

B: Yes, I don't like c _ _ _ _ _ _ _ or o _ _ _ _ _ _.
(s t a r c o r / n o o n s i)

Unit 8: Universal Design

代名詞

Reading Step 1　Getting the Picture

A 英文を読んで、話の流れに合うように下の絵を並べましょう。

CheckLink　DL 30　CD1-30

Have you ever heard of Universal Design? It is the designing of products, spaces and buildings that everyone can use. This includes older people and people with disabilities. Today, we can find examples of Universal Design products everywhere—the easy-to-open canned drinks that we buy, the ticket machines that talk to us, the low elevator buttons that children and people in wheelchairs can easily push. And let us not forget the TV remote control. What would we do without it?

Notes　disability「身体障がい」/ wheelchair「車いす」

1 ☐ → 2 ☐ → 3 ☐ → 4 ☐

a.

b.

c.

d.

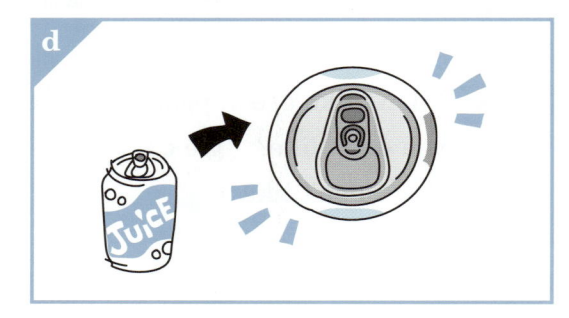

Reading Step 2 — Grammar Made Easy

代名詞 1

自分自身や相手のことを表したり、すでに出た名詞を言い換えたい場合は、代名詞を使います。

人称	格	主格（文中で主語になるもの） 「…は、…が」	目的格（文中で目的語になるもの） 「…を、…に」
一人称	単数	I	me
	複数	we	us
二人称	単数	you	you
	複数	you	you
三人称	単数	he/she/it	him/her/it
	複数	they	them

代名詞は文中での働きによって、次のように形が変化します。

I am Robert. Please call **me** Bob.　　私はロバートです。私をボブと呼んでください。
Ai is very kind. I like **her** very much.　　アイはとても親切です。私は彼女のことを大好きです。

LOOK BACK もう一度、Reading Step 1の英文を読んで、代名詞に下線を引きましょう。1つ目は1行目の <u>you</u> です。あと7つ見つけられますか。

A （　）内のa〜cから適当な語句を選び、○で囲みましょう。

1. Mr. Brown is my English teacher. (a. He　b. She　c. It) is very funny.
2. Hana is looking for her keys. She can't find (a. it　b. they　c. them).
3. Brad and I are best friends. (a. They　b. You　c. We) play golf together.
4. Lisa's boyfriend is really handsome. That's (a. he　b. him　c. they) over there.
5. Look at Megumi's sunglasses. (a. It's　b. He's　c. They're) so cool!

B 英文を読んで、空所に適当な代名詞を入れましょう。その後で音声を聞いて答えを確認しましょう。

DL 31　CD1-31

Hi. I'm Sandra. I'm a university student. ＿ am studying fashion design. ＿ is really interesting. Our teachers are very good, but ＿ give a lot of homework.

代名詞 2

人について、「…の」「…のもの」「…自身」と言いたい場合も、代名詞を使って表すことができます。

人称	格	所有格 「…の」	所有代名詞 「…のもの」	再帰代名詞 「…自身」
一人称	単数	my	mine	myself
	複数	our	ours	ourselves
二人称	単数	your	yours	yourself
	複数			yourselves
三人称	単数	his	his	himself
		her	hers	herself
		its	—	itself
	複数	their	theirs	themselves

これらの代名詞も文中での働きによって、次のように形が変化します。

My brother is 30 years old.	私の弟は30歳です。
This racket is **yours**, not **mine**.	このラケットはあなたのもので、私のものではありません。
Please introduce **yourself**.	自己紹介をしてください（＝あなた自身を紹介してください）。

C （　）内のa〜cから適当な語句を選び、○で囲みましょう。

1. My apartment is near the university. Where's (**a.** you　**b.** your　**c.** yours)?
2. Tom is very talented. (**a.** His　**b.** He　**c.** He's) hobby is painting.
3. Chiemi has a cat. (**a.** It　**b.** Its　**c.** It's) name is Coco.
4. Sally and I really enjoyed (**a.** us　**b.** myself　**c.** ourselves) in New York.
5. Mary and (**a.** his　**b.** her　**c.** their) husband have twin girls.

D 日本語を参考に、会話文を完成させましょう。その後で音声を聞いて答えを確認しましょう。

DL 32　　CD1-32

1. **A:** These keys aren't _____. [私のもの]
   B: Ask Jim. Maybe they're _____. [彼のもの]
2. **A:** I love the painting in your living room. Did you paint it _____? [あなた自身で]
   B: No, Danny painted it. He gave it to me for _____ birthday. [私の]

Reading Step 3 Getting the Idea

A (　)内のa〜bから適当な語句を選び、英文を完成させましょう。その後で音声を聞いて答えを確認しましょう。

CheckLink　DL 33　CD1-33

　Every year millions of people of all ages, abilities and nationalities pass through Japan's airports. In recent years, Universal Design ideas have been used to make its airports better. A good example is the international terminal of Tokyo's Haneda Airport, which opened in 2010. Much thought went into the design of the restrooms. All of ¹(**a.** them **b.** us) have multifunction toilets. ²(**a.** It **b.** They) can be used by people in wheelchairs, people with other disabilities, and people with baby strollers. Automatic doors are convenient, especially for people in wheelchairs. However, they don't work well for people who need help to set ³(**a.** ourselves **b.** themselves) on the toilet. Also, it isn't easy for people with visual problems to find the buttons to open and close the doors. This was a difficult problem for the designers. Finally, ⁴(**a.** he **b.** they) decided to use very lightweight doors that open manually.

　The terminal building has many other Universal Design features. One of them is the world's first nonsloping boarding bridges. One international traveler at Haneda Airport said, "This airport is wonderful. I wish ⁵(**a.** ours **b.** yours) were designed like this."

Notes multifunction「多機能の」/ baby stroller「ベビーカー」/ manually「手で」/ feature「特徴」/ nonsloping「坂になっていない」/ boarding bridge「搭乗ブリッジ」

B もう一度英文を読み、1〜4の英文について適切な語句を選びましょう。

1. The designers used lightweight toilet doors (**a.** for easy opening   **b.** to save money   **c.** because they are very strong).
2. The toilet doors open (**a.** automatically   **b.** by pushing a button   **c.** manually).
3. Haneda airport is the first airport in the world to have (**a.** multifunctional toilets   **b.** boarding bridges with no slopes   **c.** Universal Design features).
4. The traveler thinks the airports in his country are (**a.** designed like   **b.** better than   **c.** not like) Haneda Airport.

Fun with Words ▶ Noun Combinations

A 例にならい、名詞と名詞を組み合わせて1つの名詞を作ってみましょう。左側は2語で1つの名詞に、右側は2つの名詞が1つに組み合わさります。

Separated
album   center   ~~clock~~   coat
dancer   dressing   game
jam   shop   stop

Unseparated
belt   book   brush   burger
chain   cycle   phones   ship
store   ~~tub~~

1. alarm _clock_
2. ballet _____
3. bus _____
4. coffee _____
5. computer _____
6. photo _____
7. salad _____
8. shopping _____
9. strawberry _____
10. winter _____

11. bath_tub_
12. cheese _____
13. drug _____
14. head _____
15. key _____
16. motor _____
17. note _____
18. seat _____
19. space _____
20. tooth _____

B **A**を参考にして、例を2つずつ作ってみましょう。

1. _____   3. _____
2. _____   4. _____

Mars One

will/be going to

Unit 9

Reading Step 1 — Getting the Picture

A 英文を読んで、話の流れに合うように下の絵を並べましょう。

CheckLink　DL 34　CD1-34

Imagine someone said to you, "We are going to send people to Mars and they are going to live there for the rest of their lives. They're going to wear regular clothes, grow vegetables, cook and take hot showers. But they are never going to return to Earth." In fact, that is what Mars One is going to do. The Dutch foundation Mars One plans on sending humans to live on Mars by the year 2023. Thousands of would-be astronauts have already applied for the job.

Notes ▶ Mars「火星」/ Dutch「オランダの」/ foundation「財団法人」/ would-be「…志望の」/ astronaut「宇宙飛行士」/ apply「申し込む」

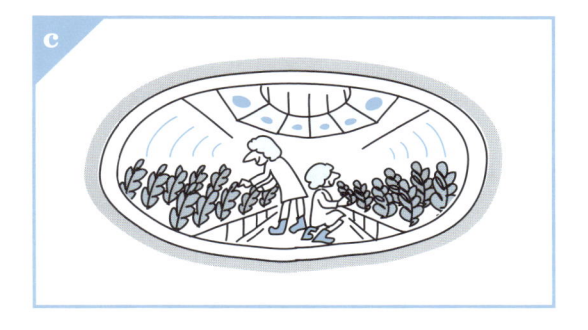

1 ☐ → 2 ☐ → 3 ☐ → 4 ☐

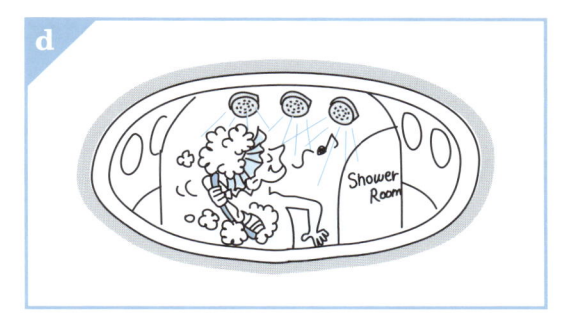

Reading Step 2　Grammar Made Easy

be going to を使った未来表現

「すでに決まっている予定」や「確実に起こりそうなこと」を表現したい場合は、主語の後に〈be動詞＋going to＋動詞の原形〉を続けます。

| My sister **is going to** visit Kyoto next month. | 私の姉は来月、京都を訪れる予定です。 |
| Look at those black clouds. It **is going to** rain soon. | あの黒い雲を見て。もうすぐ雨が降るでしょう。 |

否定文を作るときは、be動詞の後ろにnotをつけます。また、疑問文を作るときは、主語の前にbe動詞を置きます。

| **I'm not going to** change my mind. | 私は自分の考えを変えるつもりはありません。 |
| **Are** you **going to** go out tonight? | あなたは今晩、外出する予定ですか。 |

LOOK BACK もう一度 Reading Step 1の英文を読んで、be going toの後に続く動詞に下線を引きましょう。1つ目は1行目の<u>send</u>です。あと7つ見つけられますか。

A (　)内のa～cから適当な語句を選び、○で囲みましょう。

1. Natsuki (a. going　b. is going　c. is going to) study in Canada this summer.
2. Tina and I (a. am　b. is　c. are) going to see a movie tonight.
3. (a. They're not going to　b. They not going to　c. They're going to not) come.
4. It's almost 9:00. Reiko is going (a. late　b. to late　c. to be late) for class.
5. Meg and Don (a. is going to get　b. are going to get　c. going to get) married!

B 例にならい、(　)内の語句を使って、会話文を完成させましょう。その後で音声を聞いて答えを確認しましょう。

DL 35　CD1-35

1. A: <u>Are you going to work</u> today? (you / work) [今日は仕事をする予定なの？]
   B: No, ＿＿＿＿＿＿＿＿＿＿＿＿ tennis with Mike. (I / play)
   [いいや、僕はマイクとテニスをする予定だよ]

2. A: ＿＿＿＿＿＿＿＿＿＿＿＿ to Kyoto by train? (they / travel)
   [彼らは京都まで電車で行くつもりですか]
   B: Yes, ＿＿＿＿＿＿＿＿＿＿＿＿ the *Shinkansen*. (they / take)
   [はい、彼らは新幹線で行くつもりです]

willを使った未来表現

「これから起こりそうなこと」について述べたり、たずねたりしたい場合は、動詞の前にwillを置きます。その出来事が起こるかどうかが確実でないときは、be going toではなくwillを使います。

| This movie **will** become a mega hit. | この映画は大ヒットになるでしょう。 |
| My parents **will** go on an around-the-world trip after their retirement. | 私の両親は退職後に世界一周旅行をするでしょう。 |

否定文を作るときは、willの後ろにnotをつけます。通常は短縮形（won't）を使います。また、疑問文を作るときは、主語の前にwillを置きます。

| It **won't** rain this afternoon. | 今日の午後は、雨は降らないでしょう。 |
| **Will** you eat dinner at home tonight? | あなたは今晩、家で夕食を食べますか。 |

C （　）内のa〜cから適当な語句を選び、○で囲みましょう。

1. My father (**a.** will   **b.** will be   **c.** will to be) 50 years old tomorrow.
2. I'm sure you (**a.** have   **b.** will have   **c.** will having) a great time tomorrow.
3. Let's ask Yumi to keep the tickets. She (**a.** will   **b.** not   **c.** won't) lose them.
4. Take your umbrella. (**a.** It will rain   **b.** It's raining   **c.** It won't rain) later.
5. (**a.** Will you do your report   **b.** You'll your report do   **c.** Your report will do) tonight?
6. Don't worry. (**a.** You'll fail   **b.** You won't pass   **c.** You'll pass) the test.

D （　）内の語句とwillを使って、会話文を完成させましょう（短縮形にできる場合は短縮形を使います）。その後で音声を聞いて答えを確認しましょう。

1. **A:** _____ at the party on Saturday? (Kevin / be)
   B: Yes, and _____ his new girlfriend. (he / bring)
2. **A:** Watch this video. _____. (you / love / it)
   B: OK, but _____ today. (I / not / have / time)

Reading Step 3 Getting the Idea

A (　　)内のa～bから適当な語句を選び、英文を完成させましょう。その後で音声を聞いて答えを確認しましょう。

CheckLink　DL 37　CD1-37

　The organization Mars One is going to send people to live on Mars by 2023. But first, the astronauts will need eight years of training. In addition to their work as astronauts, they will ¹(**a.** learn　**b.** teach) many new skills. They include how to grow food, how to do repair work, and how to fix teeth and broken bones.

　The trip to Mars ²(**a.** is　**b.** isn't) going to be easy. It will take about seven months. During those seven months, the astronauts ³(**a.** will live　**b.** will play) together in a very small space, eat freeze-dried and canned food, wash their bodies with small wet towels and exercise for three hours every day. A new group of four astronauts will travel to Mars every two years, so the population will gradually increase. Eventually, they are going to ⁴(**a.** build　**b.** open) a living unit from local materials such as wood.

　Humans living on Mars ⁵(**a.** will help　**b.** will not help) us to better understand our solar system, how life began and our place in the universe. Just like the first Apollo moon landing in 1969, a human mission to Mars will inspire us to believe that anything is possible.

Notes　organization「組織、機関」/ in addition to ...「…に加えて」/ gradually「しだいに」/ eventually「最終的に」/ solar system「太陽系」/ mission「使命」

B もう一度英文を読み、1〜4の英文について適切な語句を選びましょう。

1. The Mars One astronauts will begin training (a. in eight years   b. in 2023   c. eight years before traveling to Mars).
2. During the trip to Mars, the astronauts will (a. exercise three hours a day   b. learn many new skills   c. eat fresh food).
3. A new group of astronauts will travel to Mars every (a. seven months   b. two years   c. four years).
4. The Mars One astronauts will eventually (a. return to Earth   b. travel to other places in the universe   c. grow trees on Mars).

Fun with Words ▶ Common Phrases

A 例にならい、それぞれの日本語に合うよう、動詞と名詞を組み合わせましょう。

1. 写真を撮る — take a picture
2. 友だちに会う
3. ミスをする
4. 秘密にする
5. 話をする
6. かぜをひく
7. 願いごとをする
8. 昼寝をする
9. 夢を見る
10. ウソをつく
11. 約束を守る
12. 締め切りに間に合う

[動詞]
have / have   keep / keep
make / make   meet / meet
take / take   tell / tell

[名詞]
a cold   a deadline
a dream   a friend
a lie   a mistake
a nap   a picture
a promise   a secret
a story   a wish

B 空所に入る適当な語句を **A** から選び、英文を完成させましょう。

1. I'm not going to school today because I (   ).
2. Excuse me. Could you (   ) of me with this camera?
3. I want to tell you something, but can you (   )?
4. Some companies let tired workers (   ) at their desk.

Unit 10

Getting Around

助動詞

Reading Step 1 Getting the Picture

A 英文を読んで、話の流れに合うように下の絵を並べましょう。

CheckLink DL 38 CD1-38

First-time visitors to Venice <u>may be</u> surprised that most people get around on foot. You can walk from one end of the city to the other in about an hour. The only other way to get around is by boat. Venice is, of course, famous for its gondolas. A gondola ride is very expensive, however, and most people can't afford it. For everyday travel, the *vaporetti*, or water bus, is best. If you're in a hurry, then you might want to take a *taxi acquei*, or water taxi.

Notes get around「動き回る」 / gondola「ゴンドラ」 / afford「…の金銭的余裕がある」

1 ☐ → 2 ☐ → 3 ☐ → 4 ☐

a

b

c

d

Reading Step 2 | Grammar Made Easy

助動詞 1

「…できる」「…かもしれない」のように、「能力」や「可能性」を表す意味をつけ加えたい場合は、動詞の前に助動詞のcanやmayなどを置きます。助動詞の後の動詞はつねに原形です。

can「…できる」	Michael **can** speak three languages. マイケルは3ヵ国語を話すことができます。
may「…してもよい、…かもしれない」 might「…かもしれない」	You **may** use your dictionary. あなたは辞書を使ってかまいません。 Becky **might** call you tonight. ベッキーは今晩、あなたに電話するかもしれません。
＊より可能性が低いことを表す場合はmayではなくmightを使います。	

否定文を作るときは、助動詞の後ろにnotをつけます。また、疑問文を作るときは、助動詞を主語の前に置きます。

I **can't** answer this question.	私はこの質問に答えることができません。
May I use the bathroom?	お手洗いを使ってもよいですか。

LOOK BACK もう一度 Reading Step 1 の英文を読んで、〈助動詞＋動詞の原形〉に下線を引きましょう。1つ目は1行目の <u>may be</u> です。あと3つ見つけられますか。

A （　　）内のa～cから適当な語句を選び、○で囲みましょう。

1. Alanis can (**a.** sing　**b.** sings　**c.** to sing) very well.
2. It's getting cloudy. It (**a.** can　**b.** may not　**c.** might) rain.
3. Put away your cell phone. You (**a.** could　**b.** may　**c.** might) not use it in class.
4. (**a.** May I see　**b.** See I may　**c.** I may see) your passport, please?
5. Yui (**a.** can't　**b.** may not　**c.** might not) cook, so she always eats out.

B 例にならい、（　　）内の語句とcanまたはmayを使って、英文を完成させましょう。その後で音声を聞いて答えを確認しましょう。

DL 39　CD1-39

1. I'm sorry, these seats are reserved. <u>You may not sit</u> here. (not / sit / you)
2. It's a clear night. ＿＿＿＿＿＿＿＿＿＿ in the sky. (many stars / see / you)
3. I'm hot. ＿＿＿＿＿＿＿＿＿＿, please? (I / open / the window)
4. I need my glasses. ＿＿＿＿＿＿＿＿＿＿ without them. (not / see well / I)

助動詞 2

助動詞には他にも、「義務」「必要性」、「提案」「忠告」の意味を表すものがあります。

must/have to「…しなければならない」	We **must/have to** obey the rules. 私たちは規則に従わなければなりません。
should「…すべき、当然…だ」 **ought to**「…すべき」 **had better**「…すべき、…しなさい」	You **should/ought to/had better** listen to his advice. あなたは彼の助言を聞くべきです。

＊shouldとought toは、ほぼ同じ程度の強さの提案を表しています。had betterは、より強い提案や相手に対する命令を表すときに使います。

肯定文ではmustとhave toはほぼ同じ意味で使われますが、否定文では次のように意味が変わります。

You **must not** enter this room.	あなたはこの部屋に入ってはいけません。
You **don't have to** come to the meeting.	あなたはミーティングに来る必要はありません。

C （　）内のa〜cから適当な語句を選び、○で囲みましょう。　　　CheckLink

1. At this store, you must (**a.** paying　**b.** pay　**c.** to pay) in cash.
2. Do you have (**a.** do　**b.** do to　**c.** to do) a lot of homework for this class?
3. It's late. We had (**a.** better　**b.** better to　**c.** to better) go home.
4. Take your time. You (**a.** don't have to　**b.** have to not　**c.** not have to) hurry.
5. It's cold. You ought (**a.** put on　**b.** put on to　**c.** to put on) a sweater.
6. You (**a.** must not　**b.** must to not　**c.** must not to) eat in the library.

D 例にならい、空所に入る助動詞を下から選び、（　）内の語句を使って、会話文を完成させましょう。その後で音声を聞いて答えを確認しましょう。　　　DL 40　CD1-40

~~should~~　don't have to　must　must not

1. A: I lost my textbook. What <u>should I do</u>? (I / do) ［私は何をすべきでしょうか］
   B: You have no choice. _____ a new one. (You / buy)
   ［あなたは新しいものを買わなければなりません］

2. A: I'm so happy. _____ early tomorrow. (I / get up)
   ［私は明日は早起きする必要はありません］
   B: Really? I have a test from 9:00. _____. (I / oversleep)
   ［私は寝坊してはいけません］

Reading Step 3 Getting the Idea

A (　　)内のa～bから適当な語句を選び、英文を完成させましょう。その後で音声を聞いて答えを確認しましょう。

CheckLink　DL 41　CD1-41

London is famous for its black cabs, or taxis. London cab drivers are very polite. They are also very good at their job. In order to become a cab driver in London, drivers ¹(a. might   b. must) pass a test called "The Knowledge." Since 1865, they have had to memorize all 25,000 street locations and 20,000 place names within six miles (10 km) of Charing Cross. Charing Cross is an area in Central London. It ²(a. can   b. has to) take two to four years to learn everything. To get a cab driver's license, test takers ³(a. may   b. have to) explain the best route between two points, including street names, place names and turns. Of course, they ⁴(a. can   b. may not) look at a map.

You ⁵(a. can   b. may) be surprised to learn that a London cab driver's brain changes during preparation for "The Knowledge." In fact, one part of the brain, the hippocampus, is much larger in London cab drivers than in other people, including doctors, bus drivers and memory champions. After London cab drivers retire, the hippocampus returns to its normal size.

Notes memorize「記憶する」/ location「場所、位置」/ turn「曲がり角」/ brain「脳」/ hippocampus「海馬」/ memory champion「記憶力大会のチャンピオン」/ retire「引退する」

B もう一度英文を読み、1〜4の英文について適切な語句を選びましょう。

1. There are 25,000 streets (**a.** in London **b.** in Charing Cross **c.** within six miles of Charing Cross).
2. It takes people (**a.** several years **b.** one or two years **c.** two to four months) to memorize all the streets and locations.
3. Test takers have to (**a.** drive around London without a map **b.** describe the best way to get from one point to another **c.** explain the bus route between two points).
4. The hippocampus of a London bus driver is (**a.** smaller than **b.** larger than **c.** the same size as) the hippocampus of a London cab driver.

Fun with Words ▶ Transportation

A 例にならい、それぞれの日本語に合う英語の語句を見つけてみましょう。語句は上下左右斜めに読めるものとします。

```
Z H T U B S H I P H
R E U V I Y Q I Z F
E L C Y C R O T O M
U I A D Y A W B U S
E C R C C U L R U N
O O T Y L N A S E I
S P A C E S H I P A
N T Z B F V X I J R
T E K J U A Q E L T
L R Q L T S D F I W
```

1. 自転車 _ _ _ _ _ _ _
2. バス B U S
3. 自動車 _ _ _ _
4. ヘリコプター _ _ _ _ _ _ _ _ _ _
5. オートバイ _ _ _ _ _ _ _ _ _ _
6. 船 _ _ _ _
7. 宇宙船 _ _ _ _ _ _ _ _
8. 地下鉄 _ _ _ _ _ _
9. タクシー _ _ _ _
10. 電車 _ _ _ _ _

B 空所に入る適当な語句を**A**から選び、英文を完成させましょう。

1. John rides his (_____) to school every day. It's good exercise.
2. We flew over the city by (_____). It was so fun!
3. The (_____) landed in the field, and three aliens came out.

The "Meat" of Tomorrow

形容詞

Unit 11

Reading Step 1 — Getting the Picture

A 英文を読んで、話の流れに合うように下の絵を並べましょう。

Did you know that 95% of the animals on the Earth are insects? In fact, there are more than one million kinds. Insects are small, and most of them can fly. Because of their size, they can live in tiny spaces, and they don't need a large amount of food. Some insects are harmful to humans because they eat plants or carry diseases. On the other hand, some insects are helpful to us by making honey or pollinating flowers. Others are useful as food for animals, including people.

Notes insect「昆虫」/ amount「量」/ pollinate「受粉する」

1 ☐ → 2 ☐ → 3 ☐ → 4 ☐

Reading Step 2　Grammar Made Easy

形容詞の基本用法

「赤い車」や「小さな家」のように、名詞（「車」「家」）に説明を加えたい場合は、形容詞を使います。

I want to have a **new** computer.	私は新しいコンピュータが欲しいです。
The **old** lady lives in a **small** village.	その年老いた女性は小さい村に住んでいます。

形容詞は名詞の前に置かれるだけでなく、〈主語＋be動詞（など）＋形容詞〉の形で、主語の補足説明をするときにも使います。

My smartphone is very **useful**.	私のスマートフォンはとても役に立ちます。
These flowers are **beautiful**.	これらの花々は美しいです。
My grandfather became **ill**.	私の祖父は具合が悪くなりました。

LOOK BACK もう一度 Reading Step 1 の英文を読んで、small と helpful に下線を引きましょう。その後で、この2つの形容詞と同じような意味を持った形容詞を1つずつ探して、下線を引きましょう。さらに、反対の意味を持った形容詞を1つずつ探して□で囲みましょう。

A （　）内の a～c から適当な語句を選び、○で囲みましょう。　　CheckLink

1. Peter's parents live in (a. a small town　b. small a town　c. a town small).
2. You (a. don't happy look　b. look don't happy　c. don't look happy) today.
3. Is your city (a. a safe　b. safe　c. safety)?
4. Tony's (a. wife is Japan　b. wife is Japanese　c. Japanese wife).
5. This peach is sweet and (a. juicy　b. juice　c. a juicy).
6. Your suitcase is (a. very a heavy　b. a very heavy　c. very heavy).

B 空所に入る形容詞を下から選び、英文を完成させましょう。その後で音声を聞いて答えを確認しましょう。　　DL 43　CD1-43

delicious　hot　hungry　little

Today I had lunch in a ＿＿＿＿＿＿＿ café near the station. It was a ＿＿＿＿＿＿＿ day and I wasn't very ＿＿＿＿＿＿＿, so I just ordered a salad. It was fresh and ＿＿＿＿＿＿＿.

形容詞の順番

「2人の かわいい 女の子」や「6つの 大きい 青森産の リンゴ」のように、いくつかの形容詞を一緒に使いたい場合、英語では並べる順番が決まっています。

順番	①	②	③	④	⑤	⑥	⑦
種類	数	主観的評価	大小	形・性質	新旧	色	材質・国名など
例	two three	pretty expensive	big small	long soft	new old	red yellow	wooden German

例えば、大小を表す形容詞（bigなど）と数を表す形容詞（threeなど）を同時に使う場合は、three big apples（3つの大きなリンゴ）のように、数を表す形容詞が先に来ます。

My mother bought me a ②**pretty** ③**little** ⑥**pink** bag for my birthday.
母は私の誕生日に、かわいくて小さいピンク色のバッグを買ってくれました。

Bill has ①**two** ②**expensive** ⑦**German** cars.
ビルは2台の高級なドイツ製の車を持っています。

＊丸付きの数字は上の表に対応しています。

C （　）内のa〜cから適当な語句を選び、○で囲みましょう。

1. Julia has (a. hair long blond   b. blond long hair   c. long blond hair).
2. Alice bought (a. a new cute dress   b. a cute new dress   c. cute new a dress).
3. I just downloaded (a. two new songs   b. new two songs   c. two songs new).
4. We had dinner at (a. quiet a little French   b. little a quiet French   c. a quiet little French) restaurant.
5. Sam drives (a. an expensive car German   b. an expensive German car   c. a German expensive car).
6. I have a (a. small old wooden   b. small wooden old   c. wooden old small) table.

D （　）内の形容詞を正しい順番に並べて英文を完成させましょう。その後で音声を聞いて答えを確認しましょう。

1. Steve wears _____ glasses. (black / round / small)
2. Angela has _____ boys. (cute / little / three)
3. Jim ordered _____ pizzas. (large / two / pepperoni)
4. Mari bought a _____ bag. (beautiful / brown / leather)

Reading Step 3 Getting the Idea

A (　)内のa～bから適当な語句を選び、英文を完成させましょう。その後で音声を聞いて答えを確認しましょう。

CheckLink　DL 45　CD1-45

　There are over seven billion people in the world today, and that number will reach nine billion before 2050. Between now and then, the demand for meat will double. Raising animals, however, requires ¹(**a.** small **b.** large) areas of farmland. Feeding them can be expensive. One solution is for more people to start eating insects.

　In fact, people in many parts of the world have been eating insects for thousands of years. And why not? Insects are healthy, ²(**a.** easy and cheap **b.** difficult and expensive) to raise and, according to insect eaters, ³(**a.** tasteless **b.** delicious). More than 1,700 kinds of insects are safe to eat. However, very few people in Europe, the United States and other rich countries eat insects. People in rich countries must have a chance to sample insects and to learn how to prepare them as food. Then eating insects will become more popular.

　There are several restaurants in the United States that have insect dishes on their menus. One popular ⁴(**a.** Mexico **b.** Mexican) restaurant in New York offers two ⁵(**a.** small **b.** a small) tacos filled with *chapulines*, or little grasshoppers, for about $15. They sell 10 or 15 orders a day.

Notes ▶ billion「10億（の）」/ feed「食糧を与える」/ solution「解決策」/
sample「試食する」/ chapulines「チャプリネス」/ grasshopper「バッタ」

B もう一度英文を読み、1〜4の英文について適切な語句を選びましょう。

1. The world will have (**a.** 7   **b.** 9   **c.** 16) billion people by 2050.
2. (**a.** All   **b.** Only a few   **c.** Many) insects are safe to eat.
3. Insect-eating is not popular in (**a.** poor   **b.** rich   **c.** warm) countries.
4. The word "chapulines" means (**a.** insects   **b.** little grasshoppers   **c.** tacos).

Fun with Words ▶ Word Opposites

A 反対の意味を表す形容詞を書き、クロスワードパズルを完成させましょう。

ACROSS
2. fast
4. expensive
5. narrow
6. big
7. right
9. heavy
10. difficult

DOWN
1. hot
3. long
5. strong
6. hard
8. quiet

B 日本語に合うよう、空所に入る形容詞を下から選びましょう。

busy   easy   gentle   light

1. As _____ as a lamb (小羊のようにおとなしい＝とてもおとなしい)
2. As _____ as a feather (羽毛のように軽い＝とても軽い)
3. As _____ as a bee (ハチのように忙しい＝とても忙しい)
4. As _____ as ABC (ABCのようにやさしい＝とてもやさしい)

Unit 12

Art Crime

副詞

Reading Step 1 — Getting the Picture

A 英文を読んで、話の流れに合うように下の絵を並べましょう。

CheckLink　DL 46　CD1-46

One February morning in 1994, two men <u>quietly</u> got out of their car in front of the National Gallery in Oslo, Norway. They ran to a ladder that they had carefully hidden. Then they silently leaned it against the museum wall. One man quickly climbed to the top, broke a window with a hammer, took one of the paintings and threw it down to his partner. They returned to their car and drove away. Amazingly, this world-famous painting—Edvard Munch's *The Scream*—was easily stolen by two men with a ladder.

Notes ladder「はしご」/ lean「もたれさせる」

1 ☐ → 2 ☐ → 3 ☐ → 4 ☐

a

b

c

d

Reading Step 2 Grammar Made Easy

様子や状態を表す副詞

「彼女は<u>うれしそうに</u>笑った」や「<u>驚くことに</u>、その少年はすべてを覚えていた」のように、動作が行われている様子や状態を表したい場合は、副詞を使います。様子や状態を表す副詞は語尾が -ly で終わるものが多く、文中での位置には、次のようにいくつかのパターンがあります。

目的語がない場合 ⇒ 動詞の直後	Takeshi speaks **slowly**. タケシはゆっくり話します。
目的語がある場合 ⇒ 目的語の直後	The man left the room **quietly**. その男性は静かにその部屋を出ていきました。
受動態の場合 ⇒ be 動詞と過去分詞の間	The old book was **carefully** examined. その古い本は注意深く検査されました。
文全体を修飾する場合 ⇒ 文頭	**Luckily**, he was at home when I called. 幸運にも、私が電話したとき、彼は家にいました。

＊目的語とは、動作の対象になる語のことです。

LOOK BACK もう一度 Reading Step 1 の英文を読んで、-ly で終わる副詞を見つけて下線を引きましょう。1つ目は1行目の <u>quietly</u> です。あと5つ見つけられますか。

A (　)内の a～c から適当な語句を選び、○で囲みましょう。

1. They sang (a. beauty b. beautiful c. beautifully).
2. Tadahisa goes to bed (a. late b. lately c. slowly) every day.
3. (a. Akane studies hard b. Hard Akane studies c. Akane hard studies).
4. Nick (a. plays well the piano b. plays the piano well c. the piano plays well).
5. (a. Luck b. Lucky c. Luckily), I passed the test.

B 空所に入る副詞を下から選び、英文を完成させましょう。その後で音声を聞いて答えを確認しましょう。

DL 47　CD1-47

amazingly　badly　heavily　quickly

1. Come _____! I need your help.
2. It's raining _____ and I don't have an umbrella.
3. We played _____, and we lost the game.
4. _____, no one was hurt in the accident.

頻度を表す副詞

「週末にはよく映画を見に行きます」や「たいてい朝は納豆を食べます」のように、頻度を表したい場合も、副詞を使います。文中での位置は、be動詞または助動詞の後ろか、一般動詞の前が多く、文頭や文末に来ることもあります。

always 「つねに、いつも」	I **always** bring my camera with me. 私はいつも自分のカメラを持ち歩いています。
almost always 「ほとんどいつも」	She is **almost always** late for meetings. 彼女はほとんどいつも会議に遅刻します。
usually 「たいてい」	Bob **usually** practices basketball after school. ボブはたいてい放課後にバスケットボールの練習をします。
often 「よく、しばしば」	We **often** go to the park on weekends. 私たちはよく週末に公園に行きます。
sometimes 「ときどき」	They **sometimes** have home parties. 彼らはときどきホームパーティーをします。
rarely 「めったに…ない」	Paul **rarely** eats sweets. ポールはめったに甘いものを食べません。
never 「決して…ない」	I will **never** forget your kindness. あなたのご親切を私は決して忘れないでしょう。

C （　）内のa〜cから適当な語句を選び、〇で囲みましょう。

1. (a. Eat always I   b. Eat I always   c. I always eat) a big breakfast on Sunday.
2. Kaori (a. is often late   b. late is often   c. often lates) for class.
3. Zack (a. almost is always   b. always is almost   c. is almost always) happy.
4. It (a. not often snows   b. doesn't often snow   c. snows not often) here.
5. Dai (a. rarely plays golf   b. plays rarely golf   c. rarely golf plays).
6. I (a. can't never believe   b. can never believe   c. can believe never) him.

D 例にならい、空所に適当な語句を入れて英文を完成させましょう。その後で音声を聞いて答えを確認しましょう。

DL 48　CD1-48

1. **Ai:** Do you ever sing? **Sam:** Yes, sometimes. ⇒ Sam _sometimes sings_.
2. **Ai:** Do you eat fish? **Sam:** Yes, often. ⇒ Sam _____ _____ fish.
3. **Ai:** Will you ever leave me? **Sam:** No, never. ⇒ Sam _____ _____ _____ Ai.

Reading Step 3 — Getting the Idea

A ( )内のa～bから適当な語句を選び、英文を完成させましょう。その後で音声を聞いて答えを確認しましょう。

CheckLink　DL 49　CD1-49

Art crime is big business. Although great works such as Leonardo da Vinci's *Mona Lisa* and Edvard Munch's *The Scream* have been stolen over the years, art thieves 1(a. often   b. rarely) try to steal masterpieces nowadays. One reason is because masterpieces are 2(a. almost always   b. never) under tight security. The main reason, though, is because they are difficult to sell.

Most art thieves steal art from private homes, churches, or castles, which often have poor security systems, or none at all. For example, in 2003 two men at Scotland's Drumlanrig Castle 3(a. easily   b. unsuccessfully) overpowered a poor student guide with a knife and took a da Vinci painting. With the alarms ringing loudly, they escaped through a window and started running for their car. Two tourists from New Zealand were outside and saw everything. As the thieves were running past them, one of them said, "Don't worry, love, we're the police. This is just practice." 4(a. Luckily   b. Unhappily), the painting was found three years later. Most stolen paintings, however, are 5(a. usually   b. never) found. Around 90% of them will disappear forever.

Notes art crime「美術犯罪」/ thief「泥棒」(複数形はthieves) / masterpiece「傑作」/ overpower「取り押さえる」/ love「きみ」(呼びかけに用いられる)

B もう一度英文を読み、1〜4の英文について適切な語句を選びましょう。

1. The biggest reason why masterpieces are not stolen very often is because (**a.** most are in museums   **b.** security is very good   **c.** it is hard to find buyers).
2. (**a.** A student with a knife   **b.** Two men   **c.** New Zealand tourists) stole the da Vinci painting from Drumlanrig Castle.
3. The person running with the da Vinci painting was (**a.** an actor   **b.** a police officer   **c.** a thief).
4. About 10 percent of stolen paintings (**a.** are found   **b.** are lost forever   **c.** disappear for a few years).

Fun with Words ▶ Tools and Things

A 1〜8のイラストに合う道具をa〜hから選びましょう。

1. (　)
2. (　)
3. (　)
4. (　)
5. (　)
6. (　)
7. (　)
8. (　)

a. hammer   **b.** ladder   **c.** nail   **d.** paintbrush
e. pliers   **f.** saw   **g.** screwdriver   **h.** wrench

B 空所に入る適当な語句を **A** から選び、英文を完成させましょう。

1. I need a (　　　　　) to take out this screw.
2. Be careful not to fall off the (　　　　　).
3. Hit the nail with this (　　　　　).
4. Jack used a (　　　　　) to cut down the tree.

Do Animals Know Things We Don't Know?

Unit 13

時を表す前置詞

Reading Step 1 Getting the Picture

A 英文を読んで、話の流れに合うように下の絵を並べましょう。

CheckLink　DL 50　CD2-01

Many people in the United States and Canada celebrate Groundhog Day. Groundhog Day was first celebrated in 1886 in Punxsutawney, Pennsylvania. Every year on February 2, people gather at Gobbler's Knob at 7:25 in the morning. They wait there for Phil, the official Punxsutawney groundhog, to pop its head out of its hole. If Phil sees his shadow, he becomes afraid and goes back into his hole. This means that winter will last for six more weeks. If he doesn't see his shadow, it means that there will be an early spring.

Notes groundhog「グラウンドホッグ」(地リスの一種) / pop「飛び出す」

1 ☐ → 2 ☐ → 3 ☐ → 4 ☐

a

b

c

d

71

Reading Step 2 Grammar Made Easy

時を表す前置詞 1

「…の後に」「…までに」というように、「時」を表したい場合には前置詞を使います。前置詞の後ろには名詞が続きます。時を表す基本的な前置詞には次のようなものがあります。

in 「(年、月、午前、午後など)に」	My sister is going to marry **in** June. 私の姉は6月に結婚する予定です。
on 「(日付、曜日)に」	Let's go to a movie **on** Sunday. 日曜日に映画に行きましょう。
at 「(時刻、時間帯)に」	Please meet me at the station **at** 10:00. 駅で10時に会いましょう。
for 「(期間)の間」	I have worked in Canada **for** three years. 私はカナダで3年間、働いています。

LOOK BACK もう一度 Reading Step 1 の英文を読んで、前置詞をともなう時を表す表現に下線を引きましょう。1つ目は in 1886 です。あと4つ見つけられますか。

A ( )内のa〜bから適当な語句を選び、○で囲みましょう。

1. Karen started taking dance lessons ¹(a. in   b. on) September. They are ²(a. on   b. at) Mondays. They start ³(a. at   b. on) 7:00 p.m. and last ⁴(a. at   b. for) two hours.

2. ¹(a. In   b. On) summer, Bob gets up early ²(a. in   b. at) the morning and goes jogging ³(a. in   b. for) about 30 minutes. ⁴(a. On   b. For) holidays he goes again ⁵(a. in   b. at) night.

B 例にならい、in、on、at、for のいずれかを空所に入れて、英文を完成させましょう。その後で音声を聞いて答えを確認しましょう。

DL 51 CD2-02

1. Mary was born 1996. Her birthday is Christmas Day.
2. Chiemi is going to Boston _in_ August. She's going 10 days.
3. Bob went to Hawaii a week. Karen told me yesterday lunchtime.

時を表す前置詞 2

時を表す他の前置詞の例も見てみましょう。いずれの場合も前置詞の後ろには名詞が続きます。

before 「(時間、時期)…の前に」	I usually read the newspaper **before** breakfast. 私はいつも朝食の前に新聞を読みます。
after 「…の後に」	Shall we go out for dinner **after** work? 仕事の後に夕食を食べに行きませんか。
around 「(時間、時期)ごろ」	My father came home **around** midnight. 私の父は深夜ごろ帰宅しました。
from ... to ~ 「…から~まで」	I have to work **from** 6 **to** 10 this evening. 今晩は6時から10時まで働かなくてはなりません。
since 「(過去のある時点)以来」	I've known him **since** my high school days. 彼のことは高校のときから知っています。
by 「(期限、締切)までに」	I have to hand in this report **by** tomorrow. このレポートを明日までに提出しなければなりません。
until 「(期間の終わり)までずっと」	He'll stay in Japan **until** this weekend. 彼は今週末までずっと日本に滞在しています。
during 「(特定の期間)の間」	She kept talking **during** the meeting. 彼女はその会議の間、ずっとしゃべり続けていました。

C ( ) 内のa~cから適当な語句を選び、○で囲みましょう。

1. Let's study ¹(**a.** by **b.** during **c.** for) a few hours ²(**a.** before **b.** by **c.** on) the test.

2. Asuka took driving lessons ¹(**a.** at **b.** in **c.** on) August ²(**a.** during **b.** from **c.** since) 4 to 6 p.m.

3. Ken works late ¹(**a.** on **b.** in **c.** for) weekends and doesn't get home ²(**a.** during **b.** for **c.** until) midnight.

D 日本語を参考に、会話文を完成させましょう。その後で音声を聞いて答えを確認しましょう。

DL 52　CD2-03

1. **A:** Ryo fell asleep _____ . ［テストの間］
   B: Yes, and he must do some extra homework _____ .
   ［金曜日までに］

2. **A:** I haven't seen Jane _____ . ［昨日から］
   B: She will be here _____ . ［ランチタイムごろ］

Reading Step 3 Getting the Idea

A ( )内のa〜bから適当な語句を選び、英文を完成させましょう。その後で音声を聞いて答えを確認しましょう。

CheckLink　DL 53　CD2-04

Do animals have a sixth sense that warns them against natural disasters? ¹(**a.** For **b.** In) many years, scientists have studied animals to try to answer this question. Strange animal behavior before disasters is nothing new. A good example is the Indian Ocean Tsunami ²(**a.** for **b.** in) 2004, in which 230,000 people died. In India and Sri Lanka, dogs refused to go on their usual morning walk with their owners. Elephants ran for higher ground, and flamingos flew far away from their nests—not ³(**a.** until **b.** during) the tsunami, but well before it happened. Yala National Park in Sri Lanka reported few animal deaths ⁴(**a.** after **b.** before) the disaster.

Some scientists believe that animals sensed the danger much earlier than humans did. Others are not so sure. Scientists do agree, though, that animals can feel and smell things that humans cannot. Dogs, for example, may be able to smell a change in the air ⁵(**a.** before **b.** after) a natural disaster. Whether animals have a sixth sense remains a mystery. They do, however, seem to prepare well for natural disasters.

Notes　sixth sense「第六感」/ warn「警告する」/ natural disaster「自然災害」/ behavior「ふるまい、行動」/ refuse「拒否する」/ sense「感知する」

Do Animals Know Things We Don't Know? Unit 13

B もう一度英文を読み、1〜4の英文について適切な語句を選びましょう。　CheckLink

1. Scientists first started studying animals to find out if they have a sixth sense (**a.** a long time ago   **b.** in 2004   **c.** a few years ago).
2. Before the Indian Ocean Tsunami (**a.** dogs didn't want to leave their homes   **b.** elephants jumped up and down   **c.** flamingos flew above their nests).
3. (**a.** No   **b.** Not many   **c.** Several hundred) wild animals died in the 2004 Indian Ocean Tsunami.
4. Scientists (**a.** know that   **b.** don't believe that   **c.** disagree about whether) animals sensed danger before humans did.

Fun with Words ▶ Natural Disasters

A 例にならい、単語に合う定義を a 〜 h から選びましょう。　CheckLink

1. drought   (e)
2. earthquake   (   )
3. flood   (   )
4. landslide   (   )
5. tornado   (   )
6. tsunami   (   )
7. typhoon   (   )
8. wildfire   (   )

    a. a sudden, violent shaking of the ground
    b. very strong winds moving in a circle
    c. a very large wave in the sea
    d. earth or rocks quickly moving down a mountain or hill
    e. a long period of time with little or no rain
    f. a fire burning in a forest, grassy area, etc.
    g. a large amount of water in a place that is usually dry
    h. very strong winds and heavy rain

B 空所に入る適語を **A** のリストから選び、書き込みましょう。

1. There was a big earthquake, and the (　　　　　　　) that followed reached land several hours later.
2. The (　　　　　　　) burned for more than two weeks.

Unit 14

Godiva—The Chocolate and the Lady

場所を表す前置詞

Reading Step 1 Getting the Picture

A 英文を読んで、話の流れに合うように下の絵を並べましょう。

CheckLink　DL 54　CD2-05

In 1926, Joseph Draps opened his first Godiva chocolate shop in Brussels, Belgium. The chocolate quickly became popular because of its fine quality and delicious taste. In 1958, Draps opened a boutique on a fashionable Paris street called Rue St. Honoré. More store openings followed in other European countries. In 1966, Godiva expanded to the United States and opened a shop at Wanamaker's Department Store in Philadelphia. Six years later, a shop opened on fashionable Fifth Avenue in New York. The first Godiva shop in Asia opened in Tokyo in 1972.

Notes boutique「ブティック、専門店」/ Rue St. Honoré「サントノーレ通り」

1 ☐ → 2 ☐ → 3 ☐ → 4 ☐

Reading Step 2 — Grammar Made Easy

場所を表す前置詞 １

「…の中に」「…の上に」というように、「場所」を表したい場合は、前置詞を使います。前置詞の後ろには名詞が続きます。場所を表す基本的な前置詞には次のようなものがあります。

in 「(建物・空間・地域や国)の中に、で」	Let's swim **in** the sea this afternoon. 今日の午後、海で泳ぎましょう。
on 「(物・床や壁・通り)の上に、で」	The cat is sitting **on** the floor. その猫は床の上に座っています。
at 「(ある地点・場所)で」	I met Jeff **at** the bus stop yesterday. 昨日、バス停でジェフに会いました。
to 「(到達点)へ、に、まで」	We'll take him **to** the hospital at once. 私たちは彼を今すぐ病院に連れていきます。

LOOK BACK もう一度 Reading Step 1 の英文を読んで、場所を表す前置詞に下線を引きましょう。1つ目は1行目の <u>in</u> です。あと9つ見つけられますか。

A （　）内の a〜d から適当な語句を選び、○で囲みましょう。　　CheckLink

1. Beyoncé was born (a. in   b. on   c. at   d. to) Houston, Texas.
2. Patricia goes (a. in   b. on   c. at   d. to) Hawaii every year for vacation.
3. Let's meet (a. in   b. on   c. at   d. to) the fountain in the park.
4. The newspaper is (a. in   b. on   c. at   d. to) the chair.
5. How many students are (a. in   b. on   c. at   d. to) your class?
6. This train doesn't stop (a. in   b. on   c. at   d. to) the next station.

B 例にならい、in、on、at、to を空所に入れて、英文を完成させましょう。その後で音声を聞いて答えを確認しましょう。

DL 55　　CD2-06

1. Dave lives ˬ a big apartment building ˬ the 20th floor.
2. Mana and I went ˬ*in* the beach and swam ˬ the sea.
3. My teacher wasn't ˬ school when I went to see him, so I put my report ˬ his desk.

場所を表す前置詞 2

場所を表す前置詞の他の例も見てみましょう。いずれの場合も前置詞の後ろには名詞が続きます。

through 「(場所)を通って、通り抜けて」	The boy walked **through** the park. その少年は公園を歩いて通り抜けました。
off 「(場所や乗り物)から離れて」	We'll get **off** the train soon. 私たちはまもなく電車を降ります。
out of 「(空間・場所)から外に」	She took some money **out of** her pocket. 彼女はポケットからお金を出しました。
around 「(人・場所)のまわりに、で」	We walked **around** the lake in 40 minutes. 私たちは40分で湖のまわりを歩きました。
by 「(人・場所)のそばに、で」	Please come and sit **by** me. こちらに来て私のそばに座って下さい。
along 「(通りや河川)に沿って」	There are many cherry trees **along** the river. 川沿いにたくさんの桜の木があります。

C ( ) 内のa〜cから適当な語句を選び、〇で囲みましょう。

1. We enjoyed a nice walk (a. out of   b. through   c. along) the river.
2. Jackie fell (a. along   b. off   c. out of) her horse and broke her arm.
3. Turn on your headlights when you drive (a. through   b. by   c. along) the tunnel.
4. Put this scarf (a. by   b. along   c. around) your neck. It's cold outside.
5. I took everything (a. out of   b. off   c. by) my bag, but I couldn't find my key.
6. There's a small table (a. along   b. by   c. off) the bed.

D 空所に入る前置詞を下から選び、英文を完成させましょう。その後で音声を聞いて答えを確認しましょう。

DL 56   CD2-07

around   off   out of   through

1. I can't see _____ the window. It's too dirty.
2. Watch your step when you get _____ the train.
3. The moon travels _____ the Earth in about 27 days.
4. Please take everything _____ your locker by Friday.

Reading Step 3　Getting the Idea

A （　）内のa〜bから適当な語句を選び、英文を完成させましょう。その後で音声を聞いて答えを確認しましょう。

CheckLink　　DL 57　　CD2-08

　In the 11th century, Lady Godiva and her husband Lord Leofric lived ¹(**a.** in　**b.** to) Coventry, England. Lord Leofric was a rich and powerful man, but he gave very little to the people of his kingdom. Lady Godiva, however, cared deeply about the people, so when Lord Leofric put a high tax on them, Lady Godiva became very angry. In response, Lord Leofric told his wife that if she rode naked through the streets ²(**a.** in　**b.** on) the back of a horse, he would remove the tax. Lady Godiva quickly agreed.

　The day arrived, and Lady Godiva rode through the town on horseback, wearing only her long beautiful hair. To Lord Leofric's surprise, however, no one looked at her. Everyone stayed inside and closed their shutters. Lady Godiva finished her ride, got ³(**a.** off　**b.** on) her horse and put on her clothes. Then everyone came ⁴(**a.** into　**b.** out of) their house and gathered ⁵(**a.** along　**b.** around) her, cheering wildly. As promised, Lord Leofric removed the tax, and Lady Godiva would forever be remembered. Hundreds of years later, Joseph Draps named his chocolate company GODIVA in honor of the special lady.

Notes　Lady「夫人」(イギリス貴族の女性につける尊称) /
Lord「卿」(イギリス貴族の男性につける尊称) / kingdom「王国、王領」/
tax「税」/ in response「それに応じて」/ naked「裸の」/ remove「取り除く」/
cheer「歓声をあげる」/ in honor of ...「…に敬意を表して」

B もう一度英文を読み、1〜4の英文について適切な語句を選びましょう。　　　**CheckLink**

1. Lady Godiva was Lord Leofric's (**a.** wife   **b.** daughter   **c.** sister).
2. Lady Godiva rode naked through the town because she wanted to (**a.** show people her beauty   **b.** help the people   **c.** make her husband jealous).
3. When Lady Godiva rode through the town (**a.** everyone looked at her   **b.** everyone cheered wildly   **c.** no one saw her).
4. After Lady Godiva's ride through the town, Lord Leofric (**a.** didn't remove the tax   **b.** kept his promise   **c.** cheered wildly).

Fun with Words ▶ People Pairs

A 例にならい、それぞれの日本語に合うよう（　　）内の文字を並べ替えましょう。

1. 男の子たちと女の子たち　　boys and <u>g i r l s</u>　(s l i r g)
2. 母と父　　　　　　　　　　mother and _ _ _ _ _ _ _　(r a t h e f)
3. 男性と女性　　　　　　　　men and _ _ _ _ _ _　(m e w o n)
4. 夫と妻　　　　　　　　　　husband and _ _ _ _ _　(f e w i)
5. 淑女と紳士　　　　　　　　ladies and _ _ _ _ _ _ _ _ _　(m e t e l g e n n)
6. おばとおじ　　　　　　　　aunt and _ _ _ _ _ _　(c l u e n)
7. 息子と娘　　　　　　　　　son and _ _ _ _ _ _ _ _　(g r e a t h u d)
8. 王と女王　　　　　　　　　king and _ _ _ _ _ _　(n u q e e)
9. 王子と王女　　　　　　　　prince and _ _ _ _ _ _ _ _ _　(s p i c e r s n)
10. 花嫁と花婿　　　　　　　　bride and _ _ _ _ _ _　(m o g o r)

B 空所に入る適当な語句を **A** から選び、英文を完成させましょう。

1. After school, many (　　　　　　　　) and (　　　　　　　　　　) play in the park across the street.
2. The couple entered the church as bride and groom and left as (　　　　　　　　) and (　　　　　　　　　).

80

Aloha Hawaii

不定詞／動名詞

Unit 15

Reading Step 1 — Getting the Picture

A 英文を読んで、話の流れに合うように下の絵を並べましょう。

CheckLink　DL 58　CD2-09

Japanese love going to Hawaii for vacation. If you go, plan to go to a luau. A luau is a traditional Hawaiian barbecue party, with lots of food, entertainment and music. Before the luau begins, you can expect to receive a lei of flowers. Then you can start eating some of the many delicious foods, including roast pig, salmon, chicken and sweet potatoes. A luau also comes with traditional Polynesian entertainment. While you eat, you can enjoy watching beautiful Polynesian hula dancing and exciting fire dances.

Notes luau「ルアウ」(ハワイ語で「宴」の意味) / lei「レイ」/ Polynesian「ポリネシアの」

1 ☐ → 2 ☐ → 3 ☐ → 4 ☐

a

b

c

d

Reading Step 2 — Grammar Made Easy

不定詞と動名詞

「テニスをすることが好きです」や「音楽を聴くことを楽しみます」のように、1文中に2つ以上の動詞を使いたい場合は、不定詞 (to＋動詞の原形) や動名詞 (-ing 形) を使います。動詞によって、後ろに「不定詞が来るもの」「動名詞が来るもの」「不定詞と動名詞のどちらも来るもの」に分かれます。

後ろに不定詞が来る動詞	choose、decide、expect、need（主語が人の場合）、plan、want など I expect **to hear** from Jack. 私はジャックから連絡があることを期待しています。
後ろに動名詞が来る動詞	avoid、enjoy、finish、imagine、need（主語が物の場合）、practice など Karen enjoys **working** for this company. カレンはこの会社のために働くことを楽しんでいます。
後ろに不定詞と動名詞のどちらも来る動詞	like、love、start など I like **to play/playing** tennis. 私はテニスをすることが好きです。

LOOK BACK もう一度 Reading Step 1 の英文を読んで、〈動詞＋不定詞〉と〈動詞＋動名詞〉に下線を引きましょう。1つ目は1行目の love going です。あと4つ見つけられますか。

A （　）内の a～c から適当な語句を選び、○で囲みましょう。　CheckLink

1. Daisuke wants (a. to study　b. studying　c. どちらでもよい) English in Canada.
2. After you finish (a. to do　b. doing　c. どちらでもよい) your work, let's have tea.
3. Let's go home before it starts (a. to rain　b. raining　c. どちらでもよい).
4. We enjoyed (a. to listen　b. listening　c. どちらでもよい) to your presentation.

B 空所に入る動詞を下から選び、会話文を完成させましょう。その後で音声を聞いて答えを確認しましょう。　DL 59　CD2-10

decide　imagine　like　need

1. A: Why did you _____ to become a vegetarian, Emily?
   B: I'm not really a vegetarian. I _____ eating meat sometimes.
2. A: I can't _____ living in the country, can you?
   B: No, I _____ to be in a big city. There are so many things to do.

不定詞と動名詞で意味が変わる動詞

動詞の中には、後ろに不定詞が来る場合と動名詞が来る場合で意味が変わるものがあります。

stop	**stop＋不定詞** 「…するために立ち止まる」	John <u>stopped</u> **to take** a picture. ジョンは写真を撮るために立ち止まりました。
	stop＋動名詞 「…することを止める」	Lisa <u>stopped</u> **taking** dance lessons. リサはダンスのレッスンを受けることを止めました。
try	**try＋不定詞** 「…しようとする」	Peter <u>tried</u> **to fix** his bicycle. ピーターは自分の自転車を修理しようとしました。
	try＋動名詞 「試しに…してみる」	Mary <u>tried</u> **eating** *natto*. メアリーは試しに納豆を食べてみました。
remember	**remember＋不定詞** 「…することを忘れない」	<u>Remember</u> **to lock** the door. ドアに鍵をかけることを忘れないでね。
	remember＋動名詞 「…したことを覚えている」	I <u>remember</u> **going** to Kyoto with you. 私はあなたと一緒に京都へ行ったことを覚えています。

C (　　) 内の a～b から適当な語句を選び、○で囲みましょう。

1. It has stopped (**a.** to rain   **b.** raining). Let's go for a walk.
2. If you can't sleep at night, try (**a.** to drink   **b.** drinking) warm milk.
3. Please remember (**a.** to bring   **b.** bringing) your textbook next week.
4. I'm trying (**a.** to find   **b.** finding) my glasses. Have you seen them?
5. Let's stop (**a.** to get   **b.** getting) some gas at that service station over there.
6. I remember (**a.** to come   **b.** coming) here when I was a little boy.

D (　　) 内の動詞を不定詞か動名詞に変えて、会話文を完成させましょう。その後で音声を聞いて答えを確認しましょう。

DL 60　　CD2-11

A: Excuse me. I'm trying _____ (find) a toy for my grandson. I remember _____ (see) some here a few months ago.

B: I'm very sorry. We stopped _____ (sell) toys last week. Why don't you try _____ (look) in the store across the street. I think they have some.

Reading Step 3 — Getting the Idea

A (　)内のa～bから適当な語句を選び、英文を完成させましょう。その後で音声を聞いて答えを確認しましょう。

CheckLink　DL 61　CD2-12

　Japanese often choose ¹(**a.** to go　**b.** to swim) to Hawaii for vacation. Every year well over a million Japanese go there. About sixty per cent of them are repeat visitors. Many young couples imagine ²(**a.** getting　**b.** having) married in Hawaii or going there for their honeymoon. And why not? Hawaii has great weather, beautiful sand beaches, mountains, valleys and lovely trees and flowers. Visitors can enjoy ³(**a.** making　**b.** doing) many kinds of activities, from the usual eating and shopping, to whale watching, surfing and volcano climbing. Hawaii is also very safe, and it has good medical services with many Japanese-speaking doctors and nurses.

　One of the best things about Hawaii is the people and their "Aloha Spirit." Hawaiians are very kind and friendly people, and always stop ⁴(**a.** to ask　**b.** to help) strangers when they have questions or need assistance.

　Many Japanese students decide to combine a holiday with English study. There are many English schools in Hawaii. They can make friends with students from other countries who also want ⁵(**a.** to learn　**b.** to teach) English, and enjoy the beauty and culture of Hawaii at the same time.

Notes　repeat visitor「リピート観光客」/ whale watching「ホエールウォッチング」/ volcano「火山」/ climbing「登山」/ medical services「医療サービス」/ stranger「見知らぬ人」/ assistance「手助け」

B もう一度英文を読み、1〜4の英文について適切な語句を選びましょう。　CheckLink

1. Around (a. 40%　b. 50%　c. 60%) of the visitors to Hawaii each year have never been there before.
2. According to the passage, Hawaii has many Japanese-speaking (a. shop assistants　b. medical workers　c. tour guides).
3. Hawaiians (a. are strange people　b. like to help visitors　c. always ask strangers for assistance).
4. Many Japanese students combine (a. work with English study　b. English with cultural studies　c. a vacation with English study).

Fun with Words ▶ Natural Places

A 例にならい、それぞれの日本語に合う語句をa〜hから選びましょう。　CheckLink

1. グランドキャニオン　the Grand (b)
2. 富士山　　　　　　 (　　) Fuji
3. ナイアガラの滝　　 Niagara (　　)
4. サハラ砂漠　　　　 the Sahara (　　)
5. 琵琶湖　　　　　　 (　　) Biwa
6. ナイル川　　　　　 the Nile (　　)
7. 大西洋　　　　　　 the Atlantic (　　)
8. 日本海　　　　　　 the (　　) of Japan
9. 東京湾　　　　　　 Tokyo (　　)
10. 別府温泉　　　　　Beppu (　　)

a. Bay
b. Canyon
c. Desert
d. Falls
e. Hot Springs
f. Lake
g. Mount
h. Ocean
i. River
j. Sea

B (　) 内の文字を並べ替えて、英文を完成させましょう。最初の1文字目はあたえられています。

1. If you go to Hawaii, be sure to go swimming at Waikiki B _ _ _ _ _. (a B c e h)
2. The Rocky M _ _ _ _ _ _ _ _ are located in Canada and the U. S. (s t a i n n o M u)
3. The Galapagos I _ _ _ _ _ _ _ were made famous by Charles Darwin. (s a n d l I s)

Unit 16

Everyone Loves a Circus

現在完了

Reading Step 1 — Getting the Picture

A 英文を読んで、話の流れに合うように下の絵を並べましょう。

CheckLink　DL 62　CD2-13

Circuses have been around since the time of the Romans. And although chariot races and gladiators have disappeared from circuses, we can still see some of the acts they performed in those days, such as juggling and animal shows. Circuses have changed greatly over the years. One new kind is the contemporary circus. The contemporary circus has kept many ideas from the traditional circus. However, it has introduced new methods of presentation. For example, it often uses themes or storylines to bring together the entire performance.

Notes ▶ chariot「古代の二輪馬車（戦車）」/ gladiator「（古代ローマの）剣闘士」/ those days「当時」/ juggling「ジャグリング」/ contemporary「現代の」

1 ☐ → 2 ☐ → 3 ☐ → 4 ☐

a

b

c

d

Everyone Loves a Circus　Unit 16

Reading Step 2　Grammar Made Easy

現在完了形

「(今までに)…したことがある」「(今まで)ずっと…している」「(今は)すでに…し終わっている」などの意味をつけ加えたい場合は、現在完了形を使います。現在完了形は〈have/has＋動詞の過去分詞〉で表します。現在完了形には、よく一緒に使われることば（*）があります。

経験 「…したことがある」	*once「1回」、twice「2回」、three times「3回」 I **have read** this book twice. 私はこの本を2回読んだことがあります。
継続 「ずっと…している」	*for …「…の間」、since …「…以来」 We **have known** Jeff for 30 years. 私たちはジェフと知り合って30年になります。
完了・結果 「すでに…し終わっている」	*already「すでに」 Amy **has** already **finished** her homework. エイミーはすでに宿題をやり終えています。

LOOK BACK もう一度 Reading Step 1の英文を読んで、現在完了形に下線を引きましょう。1つ目は1行目の have been です。あと4つ見つけられますか。

A (　)内のa～cから適当な語句を選び、○で囲みましょう。

1. Debbie (**a.** has made　**b.** have made　**c.** is made) some cookies.
2. I (**a.** have see　**b.** has seen　**c.** have seen) that movie six times.
3. Donna and Andy (**a.** has gone　**b.** have went　**c.** have gone) to Las Vegas.
4. I (**a.** Ryu has known　**b.** have known Ryu　**c.** have knew Ryu) for 10 years.
5. The book has (**a.** fall　**b.** fell　**c.** fallen) off the table.

B (　)内の動詞を現在完了形に直し、会話文を完成させましょう。その後で音声を聞いて答えを確認しましょう。

DL 63　CD2-14

A: Hi. There ＿＿＿＿＿＿＿＿＿＿＿＿ (be) an accident and my train ＿＿＿＿＿＿＿＿＿＿＿＿ (stop) running.

B: What are you going to do?

A: I ＿＿＿＿＿＿＿＿＿＿＿＿ (decide) to take a bus to school. Please tell the teacher that I'll be late for class.

現在完了形の否定文と疑問文

現在完了形の否定文を作るときは、have/hasの後ろにnotをつけます。短縮形のhaven't/hasn'tが使われることもあります。また、yet（「まだ…ない」）やnever（「一度も…ない」）などがよく一緒に使われます。neverを使うときはnotは不要です。

I lost my key and I **have not** found it yet.	私はカギを失くしてしまい、まだそれを見つけていません。
We **haven't** received the letter yet.	私たちはまだその手紙を受け取っていません。
Jessica **has never** been to Japan.	ジェシカは一度も日本に行ったことがありません。

現在完了形の疑問文を作るときは、主語の前にhave/hasを置きます。already（「すでに」）、ever（「これまでに」）、before（「以前に」）、yet（「もう、すでに」）などがよく一緒に使われます。

Have you ever **seen** this movie?	あなたはこれまでにこの映画を見たことがありますか。
Has she already **eaten** lunch?	彼女はすでに昼食を食べましたか。
Have you met Bob before?	あなたは以前ボブに会ったことがありますか。

C (　)内のa〜cから適当な語句を選び、○で囲みましょう。　CheckLink

1. It (a. not has rained b. hasn't rained c. rained hasn't) for a long time.
2. (a. Have you written b. You have written c. Have written) your report yet?
3. Jack (a. has ever b. has never c. ever has) played golf.
4. (a. Already have the kids b. The kids they have already c. Have the kids already) eaten dinner?
5. I (a. have never been b. haven't never been c. never haven't been) there.
6. (a. You have ever b. You ever have c. Have you ever) climbed Mt. Fuji?

D 例にならい、(　)内の語句を使って、会話文を完成させましょう。その後で音声を聞いて答えを確認しましょう。　DL 64　CD2-15

1. A: <u>Have you studied</u> for the test? (you / study) [テストの勉強はしましたか]
   B: No, not yet. _____ time until today.
   　　　　　(I / not / have) [いいえ、まだです。私は今日まで時間がありませんでした]
2. A: _____ your parents?
   　　　　　(your boyfriend / meet) [あなたの彼氏はあなたの両親に会ったことがありますか]
   B: Actually, _____ them that I have a boyfriend.
   　　　　　(I / not / tell) [実は、私はまだ両親に彼氏がいることを話していません]

Reading Step 3　Getting the Idea

A (　　)内のa〜bから適当な語句を選び、英文を完成させましょう。その後で音声を聞いて答えを確認しましょう。

　　Have you ever seen a contemporary circus? Contemporary circuses began appearing in the 1970s and 80s in Australia, Canada, France, the United Kingdom and the United States. They have ¹(**a.** changed　**b.** seen) people's image of a circus. A contemporary circus combines traditional circus skills with modern theatrical techniques to tell a story or focus on a theme. To do this, it pays great attention to beauty and artistry through lighting, music and costume design, as well as character and story development. Contemporary circuses are often held in theaters instead of large outdoor tents. Original music is often written for each production. In recent years, animals have not ²(**a.** appeared　**b.** disappeared) very often in contemporary circuses.

　　The Canadian circus company Cirque du Soleil has ³(**a.** become　**b.** chosen) the most famous and successful contemporary circus. It has ⁴(**a.** built　**b.** grown) from 73 workers in 1984 to more than 5,000 today, including 1,300 performers. The workers and artists come from over 50 countries and speak 25 different languages. Over the years, Cirque du Soleil has thrilled audiences with its animal-free acts. More than 100 million people in over 200 cities around the world have ⁵(**a.** looked for　**b.** watched) its shows.

Notes　theatrical「演劇の」/ pay attention to ...「…に注意を払う」/ artistry「芸術性」/ as well as ...「…と同様に」/ development「発展、展開」/ instead of ...「…の代わりに」/ animal-free「動物を含まない」

B もう一度英文を読み、1〜4の英文について適切な語句を選びましょう。

1. There have been contemporary circuses (**a.** for 70 or 80 years   **b.** since the end of the last century   **c.** from Roman times).
2. One thing that does not often appear in contemporary circuses is (**a.** animal acts   **b.** original music   **c.** theatrical techniques).
3. About (**a.** 10%   **b.** 25%   **c.** 50%) of Cirque du Soleil workers are performers.
4. Cirque du Soleil has (**a.** few   **b.** free   **c.** no) animal shows.

Fun with Words ▶ Entertainment

A エンタテインメントに関する語句を書き、クロスワードパズルを完成させましょう。

ACROSS
5. a musical performance
6. an animal park
7. a game with strikes and spares
8. enjoy a meal here

DOWN
1. a popular winter sport
2. a place for swimming and surfing
3. 'empty orchestra'
4. buying or just looking?

B あたえられた文字を参考にして空所を埋め、英文を完成させましょう。

1. Tokyo Disneyland is a very popular __m__ s__ m____nt p_____.
2. Let's go to the b_____ b_____ g_____ between the Giants and the Tigers.

Text Messaging

too/enough

Unit 17

Reading Step 1 — Getting the Picture

A 英文を読んで、話の流れに合うように下の絵を並べましょう。

It is not unusual for people to exchange 60 or more text messages a day. However, exchanging <u>too many text messages</u> can be a bad thing. Too much time texting often leads to lack of concentration and poor grades in school. Too many people text while driving, and this can cause accidents. When people are too focused on their phone during classes, meetings, dates, etc., they show a lack of manners. Finally, many people text late into the night and are too tired to get up in the morning.

Notes unusual「普通でない」/ text message「携帯メール」/ exchange「やりとりする」/ lack of ...「…が欠けている」/ concentration「集中力」/ grade「成績」/ focused「集中した」/ late into the night「夜遅くまで」

1 ☐ → 2 ☐ → 3 ☐ → 4 ☐

Reading Step 2　Grammar Made Easy

too を使った表現

「この道は車が多すぎる」や「この箱は重すぎて持ち上げられない」のように、「…すぎる」という意味を表したい場合は、too を使います。使い方には、次のようなものがあります。

too＋many＋数えられる名詞	There are **too many people** in the room. 部屋には多すぎる人がいます。
too＋much＋数えられない名詞	**Too much salt** is not good for the health. 多すぎる塩分は健康によくありません。
too＋形容詞/副詞	This curry is **too hot** for me. このカレーは私には辛すぎます。 We arrived at the station **too early**. 私たちは駅に着くのが早すぎました。
too＋形容詞/副詞＋不定詞	This bag is **too heavy to carry**. このカバンは重すぎて運べません。

LOOK BACK　もう一度 Reading Step 1の英文を読んで、too を使った表現すべてに下線を引きましょう。1つ目は2行目の too many text messages です。あと4つ見つけられますか。

A （　）内のa～cから適当な語句を選び、○で囲みましょう。　CheckLink

1. You bought (a. too many vegetable　b. too much vegetables　c. too many vegetables).
2. I don't want to go out. I'm (a. too tired　b. too much tired　c. tired too much).
3. It's (a. too hot for play　b. too hot to play　c. too hot play) tennis today.
4. We have (a. too much work　b. too many work　c. too many works) this week.

B 例にならい、（　）内の語句に too をつけて、英文を完成させましょう。その後で音声を聞いて答えを確認しましょう。

DL 67　　CD2-18

1. My boss got angry at me. He said I make _too many mistakes_. (mistakes)
2. Do you like the curry, or is it _____? (spicy)
3. Please be quiet. You're making _____. (noise)
4. I couldn't finish the test. There were _____. (questions)

enoughを使った表現

「この船には十分な救命具がある」や「この説明書は十分にやさしく書かれている」のように、「十分…です」という意味を表したい場合は、enoughを使います。

enough＋数えられる名詞	There are **enough chairs** in this room. この部屋には十分なイスがあります。
enough＋数えられない名詞	Do we have **enough water** for our hike? 私たちはハイキングに十分な水がありますか。
形容詞/副詞＋enough	This room is **warm enough** for me. 私にとってこの部屋は十分に暖かいです。 You haven't practiced **hard enough**. あなたはまだ十分に熱心には練習していません。
形容詞/副詞＋enough＋不定詞	You are **old enough to get** a driver's license. あなたは運転免許を取るのに十分な年齢です。

C （　）内のa〜cから適当な語句を選び、○で囲みましょう。

1. Do we (**a.** enough money　**b.** have enough money　**c.** have money enough) for lunch?
2. We (**a.** had not enough　**b.** didn't enough　**c.** didn't have enough) time to go shopping.
3. I made (**a.** enough hotdog　**b.** hotdogs enough　**c.** enough hotdogs) for everyone.
4. He (**a.** isn't old enough　**b.** isn't enough old　**c.** is old not enough) to stay home alone.
5. Did we buy (**a.** meat enough　**b.** enough meat　**c.** enough meats) for the barbecue?

D 例にならい、（　）内の語句とenoughを使って、英文を完成させましょう（enoughの位置に注意してください）。その後で音声を聞いて答えを確認しましょう。

1. Do we have <u>enough eggs</u> to make Ron's birthday cake? (eggs)
2. Misa won't pass the test. She didn't study _____. (hard)
3. This pizza is good, but there isn't _____ on it. (cheese)
4. Are you _____, or shall I turn on the air conditioner? (warm)

Reading Step 3 Getting the Idea

A (　　)内のa〜bから適当な語句を選び、英文を完成させましょう。その後で音声を聞いて答えを確認しましょう。

CheckLink　DL 69　CD2-20

　Many people are addicted to their cell phones and take them to bed with them. Is it possible that they are texting while they are sleeping? Some experts say yes. They also believe that there is ¹(**a.** enough　**b.** not enough) information to suggest that it is becoming more common.

　A cell phone beep is loud enough to lightly wake up a sleeping person. When this happens, the person may text a message (which often makes no sense). The person then quickly falls asleep again, and remembers nothing in the morning. People usually learn about their sleep texting from friends. Sometimes friends tell them that their messages weren't ²(**a.** too clear　**b.** clear enough) to understand. Other times friends actually show them the messages that they received.

　Experts believe that not getting ³(**a.** too much　**b.** enough) sleep can leave people in a half-asleep, half-awake state. This makes it possible to answer text messages without remembering later. For many people there simply aren't enough ⁴(**a.** hours　**b.** time) in a day to do everything they need to do. They feel like they are "on call" at night. Maybe technology is making it too ⁵(**a.** easy　**b.** difficult) for us to separate our waking lives and sleeping lives.

Notes ▶ addicted「中毒になっている、やみつきになっている」/ beep「ピーッという音、ビープ音」/ make no sense「意味をなさない」/ on call「待機して」/ separate「分ける」

B もう一度英文を読み、1〜4の英文について適切な語句を選びましょう。　CheckLink

1. With sleep texting, people (a. don't remember sending messages   b. forget to send messages   c. send messages to themselves).
2. People may do sleep texting because they (a. have a lot of free time   b. prefer texting at night   c. do not get enough hours of sleep).
3. Sleep-texting messages are often (a. sent to the wrong person   b. impossible to understand   c. written just before a person goes to bed).
4. People sometimes find out that they are sleep texting by (a. looking at the messages they sent   b. asking friends if they received strange messages   c. dreaming about it).

Fun with Words ▶ Emoticons (Emoji)

A 例にならい、それぞれの絵文字に合う意味をa〜hから選びましょう。　CheckLink

1. (^_^)   (c)
2. (>_<)>   (   )
3. (ToT)   (   )
4. m(_ _)m (   )
5. (^^;)   (   )
6. (≧∇≦)/ (   )
7. (ー□ー;) (   )
8. (ーー;)   (   )

a. I'm sorry.   b. I'm crying.   c. I'm laughing.   d. I'm so happy.
e. I'm shy.   f. I'm surprised.   g. I'm troubled.   h. I'm worried.

B 絵文字を3つ書き、英語で意味を書いてみましょう。

1.
2.
3.

Unit 18

What Type Are You?

句動詞／イディオム

Reading Step 1 — Getting the Picture

A 英文を読んで、話の流れに合うように下の絵を並べましょう。

CheckLink　DL 70　CD2-21

Many people in Japan believe that a person's personality is decided by his or her blood type. There are four blood types—A, B, O and AB. Blood-type A people are said to be very hard-working and kind. They care about detail. B-type people are very friendly and strong-willed. They don't worry about what others think. People with O-type blood are easygoing. They are good leaders and often look after younger people. AB-types are creative and sensitive. They like to find out new things.

Notes　personality「性格」／ strong-willed「意志が強い」／ easygoing「気楽な」／ sensitive「繊細な」

1 ☐ → 2 ☐ → 3 ☐ → 4 ☐

Reading Step 2 Grammar Made Easy

句動詞

動詞の中には、副詞や前置詞とセットになって使われるものがあります。これを句動詞と呼びます。よく使われるものを見てみましょう。

turn on「…をつける」 **turn off**「…を消す」	Please **turn off** the radio and **turn on** the TV. ラジオを消して、テレビをつけてください。
find out 「…を見つける、探し出す」	How did you **find out** my address? あなたはどうやって私の住所を探し出したのですか。
put on 「…を着る、身につける」	You should **put on** your coat. あなたはコートを着るべきです。
take off 「…を脱ぐ」	You must **take off** your shoes here. ここでは靴を脱がなければなりません。
look forward to 「…を楽しみにする」	I **look forward to** your concert. あなたのコンサートを楽しみにしています。

LOOK BACK もう一度 Reading Step 1の英文を読んで、句動詞に下線を引きましょう。1つ目は3行目の care about です。あと3つ見つけられますか。

A （　）内のa～cから適当な語句を選び、○で囲みましょう。

1. Please turn (a. on   b. off   c. down) your computer when you finish using it.
2. How often do you clean (a. out   b. over   c. up) your room?
3. The bananas were too old, so I had to throw them (a. about   b. after   c. away).
4. It's your birthday, so I'll pay (a. for   b. out   c. with) lunch.
5. Kumiko gets (a. along   b. over   c. up) well with her sister.

B 空所に入る適当な語句を選び、英文を完成させましょう。その後で音声を聞いて答えを確認しましょう。

DL 71　CD2-22

　　　around　away　off　on

1. If you're hot, why don't you take _____ your sweater?
2. If you want to hear the news, turn _____ the radio.
3. When I visited Boston, my friend showed me _____ the city.
4. Some of my clothes were too small, so I gave them _____ .

イディオム

句動詞以外にも、動詞が他の語句とセットになって使われることがあります。これをイディオムと呼びます。ここではbe動詞を使ったイディオムを見てみましょう。

be good [bad] at … 「…が得意、上手[下手]である」	Susan **is good at** dancing. スーザンは踊ることが得意です。
be interested in … 「…に興味がある」	I **am interested in** European history. 私はヨーロッパの歴史に興味があります。
be well known for … **be famous for …** 「…でよく知られている、有名である」	Nara **is well known for** old temples and shrines. 奈良は古い神社仏閣でよく知られています。
be afraid of … 「…を恐れている」	Don't **be afraid of** making mistakes. 間違いを犯すことを恐れてはいけません。
be crazy about … 「…に夢中である」	My brother **is crazy about** heavy metal music. 私の兄はヘビメタに夢中です。
be crowded with … 「…で混雑している」	The train **is crowded with** people going home. その電車は帰宅する人々で混雑しています。

C （　）内のa〜cから適当な語句を選び、○で囲みましょう。

1. Mario is crazy (**a.** about **b.** for **c.** with) Japanese *anime*.
2. What kind of music are you interested (**a.** to **b.** in **c.** of)?
3. I like bowling, but I'm really bad (**a.** at **b.** in **c.** about) it.
4. What is your hometown famous (**a.** about **b.** with **c.** for)?
5. This market is crowded (**a.** for **b.** with **c.** to) people on Sundays.
6. Naomi is married (**a.** for **b.** with **c.** to) an American.

D 空所に入る適当な語句を選び、英文を完成させましょう。その後で音声を聞いて答えを確認しましょう。

　　about　at　of　on

1. You have studied a lot for the test. What are you worried _____?
2. Mr. and Mrs. McDonald are very proud _____ their children.
3. I'm not very keen _____ going to the party.
4. Adam is a really good tennis player. What sport are you good _____?

Reading Step 3　Getting the Idea

A (　　)内のa〜bから適当な語句を選び、英文を完成させましょう。その後で音声を聞いて答えを確認しましょう。

CheckLink　DL 73　CD2-24

　Many foreigners are surprised when they come to Japan and people ask them ¹(**a.** about　**b.** with) their blood type. Most Japanese know their own blood type, and many are good ²(**a.** at　**b.** for) guessing another person's blood type. Outside of Asia, however, not many people are interested ³(**a.** to　**b.** in) blood types. In fact, a lot of people don't even know what their blood type is.

　Though there is no scientific relationship between blood type and personality, it remains a popular subject in Japan. Morning television shows, newspapers and magazines are well known ⁴(**a.** about　**b.** for) showing blood type horoscopes. Popular *anime, manga* and video games often mention a character's blood type. Some companies make products for each blood type, such as soft drinks, chewing gum and bath salts. Blood type ideas have also been used for more serious reasons. Many dating companies use blood type information. It often helps people who are afraid ⁵(**a.** of　**b.** on) being matched up with the wrong person. Companies have made working groups based on workers' blood types. Finally, the players on the Japanese women's softball team at the Beijing Olympics received training according to their blood type. Interestingly, the team won the gold medal.

Notes　guess「推測する、当てる」/ scientific relationship「科学的関係」/ subject「テーマ」/ horoscope「占い」/ mention「…について触れる」/ working group「作業グループ」

B もう一度英文を読み、1〜4の英文について適切な語句を選びましょう。

1. Most people (**a.** in Japan   **b.** in Asia   **c.** outside of Asia) don't know their blood type.
2. There (**a.** is a   **b.** may be a   **c.** is no) scientific connection between blood type and personality.
3. Morning TV shows often show (**a.** blood type horoscopes   **b.** announcers' blood types   **c.** the blood types of famous people).
4. The players on the women's softball team (**a.** used blood type horoscopes   **b.** were trained based on their blood type   **c.** all had the same blood type).

Fun with Words ▶ What's That Person Like?

A 1〜8の説明に合う性格や性質をa〜hから選びましょう。

A person who …
1. works hard is (   ).
2. talks a lot is (   ).
3. doesn't talk much is (   ).
4. makes people laugh is (   ).
5. always tells the truth is (   ).
6. doesn't make careless mistakes is (   ).
7. is open and nice is (   ).
8. doesn't like to do work is (   ).

a. careful
b. friendly
c. funny
d. hardworking
e. honest
f. lazy
g. quiet
h. talkative

B 空所に入る適当な語句を **A** から選び、英文を完成させましょう。

1. Mari never tells a lie. She is very (   ).
2. Jack is always telling jokes. He's a (   ) person.
3. Misa doesn't like to take chances. She's a (   ) person.
4. Kohei is a good student, and he has two part-time jobs. He's
   (   ).

Japanese Food Customs

受動態

Unit 19

Reading Step 1　Getting the Picture

A 英文を読んで、話の流れに合うように下の絵を並べましょう。

CheckLink　DL 74　CD2-25

Japanese cuisine, or *washoku*, is known to be very healthy. It is also thought to be the main reason why Japanese people live long lives. *Washoku* is based on white rice. Usually it is served with *miso* soup, or bean paste soup. Then there is a main dish, such as grilled fish. The main dish is put in the middle. Two side dishes such as boiled vegetables or tofu are usually placed beside it, along with *tsukemono*, or Japanese pickles.

Notes　cuisine「料理」/ live a long life「長生きする」/
bean paste「みそ」/ side dish「おかず」/ pickle「漬け物」

1 ☐ → 2 ☐ → 3 ☐ → 4 ☐

a

b

c

d

101

Reading Step 2 Grammar Made Easy

現在形の受動態

人や物が「…される」という受け身の意味を表したい場合は、受動態を使います。現在形の受動態は〈be 動詞の現在形（am、are、is）＋過去分詞〉で表します。

| English **is spoken** in many countries. | 英語はたくさんの国で話されています。 |

「（人・物）によって（…される）」というように、動作をする側の人や物について述べたい場合は、〈by＋（人・物）〉を加えます。

| The singer **is loved** by young people. | その歌手は若者によって愛されています。 |

現在形の受動態の否定文を作るときは、be 動詞の後ろに not をつけます。また、疑問文を作るときは、be 動詞を文頭に置いて、〈be 動詞＋主語＋過去分詞〉の語順になります。

| Smoking **isn't allowed** here. | ここでは喫煙は許されていません。 |
| **Is** this bag **sold** in the online shop? | このバッグはオンラインショップで売られていますか。 |

LOOK BACK もう一度 Reading Step 1 の英文を読んで、現在形の受動態（be 動詞＋過去分詞）に下線を引きましょう。1つ目は1行目の is known です。あと5つ見つけられますか。

A （　）内のa～cから適当な語句を選び、○で囲みましょう。　CheckLink

1. All of the furniture in this store (a. made   b. are made   c. is made) by hand.
2. The Olympic Games (a. are holding   b. are held   c. is held) every four years.
3. These cars (a. aren't sold   b. isn't selling   c. not sold) anymore.
4. What language (a. is speaking   b. are speaking   c. is spoken) in Brazil?
5. When (a. breakfast is served   b. is breakfast served   c. is served breakfast)?

B （　）内の動詞を現在形の受動態に変えて、英文を完成させましょう。その後で音声を聞いて答えを確認しましょう。

DL 75　CD2-26

1. No food or drinks _____ in the library. (allow)
   ［図書館では飲食は許されません］

2. The mail _____ every day except Sunday. (deliver)
   ［郵便は日曜日を除いて毎日届けられます］

3. When _____ the trash _____ in your city? (collect)
   ［あなたの街ではいつゴミが収集されますか］

過去形の受動態

「(過去に)…された」というように、過去形の受動態を作るときは、〈be動詞の過去形(was、were)+過去分詞〉を使います。

My bicycle **was stolen** yesterday.	昨日、私の自転車は盗まれました。
This book **was written** by Haruki Murakami.	この本は村上春樹によって書かれました。
The girl **was called** Cinderella by her family.	その少女は家族からシンデレラと呼ばれていました。

過去形の受動態の否定文を作るときは、be動詞の過去形の後ろにnotをつけます。また、疑問文を作るときは、be動詞の過去形を文頭に置いて、〈be動詞の過去形+主語+過去分詞〉の語順になります。

Jim **wasn't invited** to the party.	ジムはパーティーに招待されませんでした。
Were many people **injured** in the car accident?	その自動車事故で多くの人がケガを負わされたのですか。

C ( )内のa〜cから適当な語句を選び、○で囲みましょう。 CheckLink

1. This house (a. built   b. was built   c. was building) 150 years ago.
2. *Botchan* (a. wrote   b. was written   c. was written by) Natsume Soseki.
3. We were noisy in class, so we (a. was told   b. were told   c. told) to leave.
4. Eva and I (a. wasn't chosen   b. weren't chose   c. weren't chosen) to perform.
5. Was all (a. the food eaten   b. eaten the food   c. the food was eaten)?
6. The money (a. was hidden   b. was hiding   c. was hid) in a safe place.

D ( )内の動詞を過去形の受動態に変えて、英文を完成させましょう。その後で音声を聞いて答えを確認しましょう。できあがった英文の意味も考えてみましょう。

DL 76   CD2-27

1. The old lady _____ by a kind young man. (help)
2. Some computers in our office _____ last night. (steal)
3. The students _____ much time to study for the test. (not / give)
4. _____ this rice _____ in Japan? (grow)

Reading Step 3 Getting the Idea

A （　）内のa～bから適当な語句を選び、英文を完成させましょう。その後で音声を聞いて答えを確認しましょう。

CheckLink　DL 77　CD2-28

To eat *miso* soup in Japan, the bowl is held and the soup is eaten directly from the bowl. This custom is unique among Asian countries. In South Korea, a bowl is never ¹(**a.** eaten　**b.** lifted) off the table. It is believed to be bad manners.

Metal spoons and bowls were used in Japan until 1,200 years ago. However, the bowls were expensive and were ²(**a.** made　**b.** replaced) by wooden ones over time. Because wooden bowls do not become too hot to hold like metal bowls, spoons also disappeared, and Japanese people began to eat soup directly from the bowl. This custom is practiced even today.

When foreigners visit Japan, they are often surprised to hear Japanese people make noise when they eat soup. In Japan, soup is ³(**a.** serviced　**b.** served) very hot. To lower the temperature, it is quite natural for Japanese people to mix air and soup together. This is ⁴(**a.** done　**b.** made) by slurping. Slurping is not ⁵(**a.** allowed　**b.** followed) in most other countries. These days, many foreigners who live in Japan slurp hot soup, just like Japanese people.

Notes ▶ directly「直接、じかに」/ metal「金属（の）」/ over time「やがて」/ practice「行う」/ slurp「ズルズル音を立てる、すする」

B もう一度英文を読み、1〜4の英文について適切な語句を選びましょう。

1. Lifting a bowl off the table is acceptable in (**a.** Japan   **b.** Korea   **c.** both Japan and Korea).
2. Japan started using wooden bowls because metal bowls (**a.** were too heavy   **b.** were too hot   **c.** cost too much).
3. Soup is slurped in Japan to (**a.** make it taste better   **b.** cool it down   **c.** raise the temperature).
4. It is (**a.** common   **b.** unusual   **c.** surprising) to hear foreigners who live in Japan slurp their soup.

Fun with Words ▶ Must-Know Foods

A 1〜10の食べ物に合う語句をa〜jから選びましょう。

1. せんべい (　)　5. たこ焼き (　)　9. おかゆ (　)
2. 牛丼　 (　)　6. もち　　 (　)　10. あんこ (　)
3. おにぎり (　)　7. 大根おろし (　)
4. みそ汁　(　)　8. 漬け物　 (　)

　　a. beef bowl　**b.** grated radish　**c.** Japanese pickles
　　d. miso soup　**e.** octopus dumplings　**f.** rice ball
　　g. rice cake　**h.** rice cracker　**i.** rice porridge
　　j. sweet bean paste

B 1〜4の説明に合うように、(　)内の文字を並べ替えましょう。

1. Grilled chicken on a thin stick ⇒ y＿＿＿t＿＿＿ (a i i o k t r y)
2. Fresh slices of raw fish ⇒ s＿＿＿＿＿＿＿ (m i s h i a s)
3. Chinese style noodles in soup ⇒ ＿＿＿＿＿＿ (n e m a r)
4. Sliced beef and vegetables cooked at the table in a pan
　　　　　　　⇒ ＿＿＿＿＿＿＿＿＿ (k u s i i k a y)

105

Unit 20: Mascot Characters

5文型

Reading Step 1 Getting the Picture

A 英文を読んで、話の流れに合うように下の絵を並べましょう。

CheckLink DL 78 CD2-29

<u>*Yuru kyara* are cute and friendly mascot characters.</u> They are everywhere in Japan. They promote tourism, local products, or simply a soft, friendly image. For example, Kumamoto Prefecture has Kumamon, a black bear with big round eyes and red cheeks. Hiko-nyan promotes Hikone in Shiga Prefecture. Hiko-nyan is a white cat with a samurai helmet. The towel-making city of Imabari in Ehime Prefecture has Bary-san. It's an egg-shaped yellow bird with a towel around its body. The Tokyo Metropolitan police department has Peepo-kun, an orange character with a gray antenna and big ears.

Notes promote「宣伝する」/ tourism「観光産業」/ local products「名産品」/ prefecture「県」

1 ☐ → 2 ☐ → 3 ☐ → 4 ☐

a

b

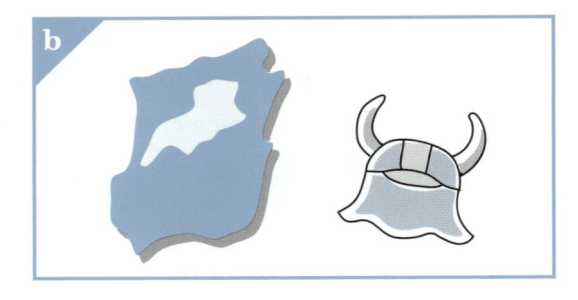

c

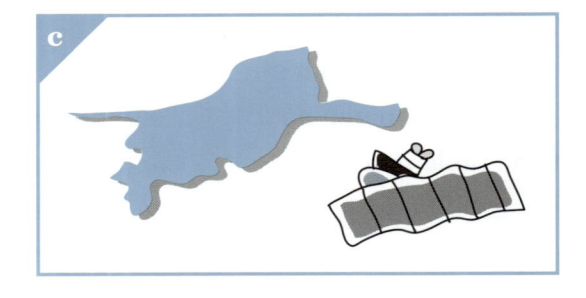

d

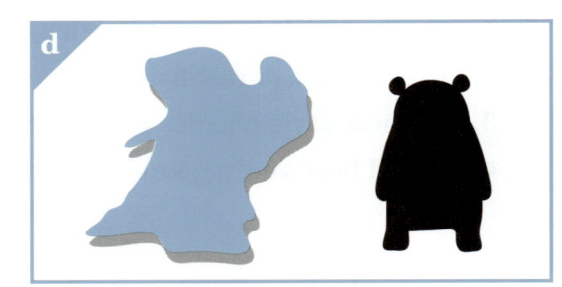

Reading Step 2　Grammar Made Easy

文型（第1文型／第2文型／第3文型）

英語の文の意味は語順で決まります。語順にはいくつかのパターンがあり、そのパターンのことを「文型」と呼びます。ここでは基本的な3つの文型を見てみましょう。Sは主語、Vは動詞、Cは補語（補足説明をする語）、Oは目的語（動作の対象になる語）を表します。

基本文型	例文
S+V 「SがVする」	**Birds sing.** 鳥たちは歌います。（SはBirds、Vはsing） **The boys cried.** 少年たちは叫びました。（SはThe boys、Vはcried）
S+V+C 「SがCである」 ＊S＝Cの関係が成り立つ	**The basketball player is tall.** そのバスケットボール選手は背が高いです。（The basketball player=tall） **My brother became a pilot.** 私の弟はパイロットになりました。（My brother=a pilot）
S+V+O 「SがOをVする」	**I made breakfast.** 私は朝食を作りました。（SはI、Vはmade、Oはbreakfast） **We play volleyball.** 私たちはバレーボールをします。（SはWe、Vはplay、Oはvolleyball）

LOOK BACK　もう一度 Reading Step 1 の英文を読んで、S＋V＋Cの文型を探して下線を引きましょう。1つ目は1行目の *Yuru kyara* are cute and friendly mascot characters. です。あと2つ見つけられますか。

A （　）内のa〜cから適当な文型を選び、○で囲みましょう。

1. Mary baked cookies. (a. S+V　b. S+V+O　c. S+V+C)
2. This soup is delicious. (a. S+V　b. S+V+O　c. S+V+C)
3. Nick is in the library. (a. S+V　b. S+V+O　c. S+V+C)
4. The kids played video games all day. (a. S+V　b. S+V+O　c. S+V+C)

B 文型を参考にして、（　）内の語句を並べ替えて、英文を完成させましょう。その後で音声を聞いて答えを確認しましょう。

　　　　DL 79　　CD2-30

1. S+V (smiled / the woman) ⇒ _____ .
2. S+V+C (fresh / smells / the bread) ⇒ _____ .
3. S+V+O (the window / opened / Danny) ⇒ _____ .

文型（第4文型／第5文型）

日本語では「父は私にプレゼントをくれた」のように「…に」「…を」という語（助詞）を使って表しますが、英語には助詞がないので、代わりに語順で文の意味を表します。

基本文型	例文
S+V+O₁+O₂ 「SがO₁にO₂をVする」	**Jeff gives me flowers.** ジェフは私に花をくれます。 （SはJeff、Vはgives、O₁はme、O₂はflowers） **Laura sent her sister a letter.** ローラは彼女の妹に手紙を送りました。 （SはLaura、Vはsent、O₁はher sister、O₂はa letter）
S+V+O+C 「SがOをCにVする」 ＊O＝Cの関係が成り立つ	**They call her Liz.** 彼らは彼女をリズと呼びます。 （SはThey、Vはcall、Oはher、CはLiz） **This song makes me happy.** この歌は私を幸せにしてくれます。 （SはThis song、Vはmakes、Oはme、Cはhappy）

C （　）内のa～bから適当な文型を選び、○で囲みましょう。　CheckLink

1. Daiki gave his girlfriend a present. (a. S+V+O+O　b. S+V+O+C)
2. We left the window open. (a. S+V+O+O　b. S+V+O+C)
3. I find Mr. Brown's class interesting. (a. S+V+O+O　b. S+V+O+C)
4. He told us a funny joke. (a. S+V+O+O　b. S+V+O+C)
5. Anne showed me some photographs of her trip. (a. S+V+O+O　b. S+V+O+C)
6. They named their baby William. (a. S+V+O+O　b. S+V+O+C)

D 文型を参考にして、（　）内の語句を並べ替えて、英文を完成させましょう。その後で音声を聞いて答えを確認しましょう。　DL 80　CD2-31

1. S+V+O+O ⇒ Yuki's mother ＿＿＿＿＿＿＿＿＿＿＿＿＿＿＿.
   (her / some money / gave)
2. S+V+O+C ⇒ I ＿＿＿＿＿＿＿＿＿＿＿＿＿＿＿.
   (find / interesting / this book)
3. S+V+O+O ⇒ Paul ＿＿＿＿＿＿＿＿＿＿＿＿＿＿＿.
   (me / sold / his computer)
4. S+V+O+C ⇒ They ＿＿＿＿＿＿＿＿＿＿＿＿＿＿＿.
   (a genius / consider / Albert)

Reading Step 3 Getting the Idea

A (　　)内のa～bから適当な語句を選び、英文を完成させましょう。その後で音声を聞いて答えを確認しましょう。

CheckLink　DL 81　CD2-32

Theme park mascots and mascots of sports teams are ¹(a. common b. a common) in many countries, including Japan. Japan, however, also has hundreds of *yuru kyara*. *Yuru kyara* means "loose character." They are usually designed to look cute and a little silly. This creates a loose, relaxed and ²(a. friendly b. friendly feeling). That is why people like them so much.

There is even a mascot school in Tokyo. It is called Choko Group. It is probably the only school in the world that trains people to become professional mascots. Choko Ohira started the school in 1985. Ms. Ohira is a veteran of wearing mascot costumes. Students ³(a. hard work b. work hard). She teaches ⁴(a. them traditional dance b. traditional dance them) and various walking styles. Students also learn how to interact with children, how to look friendly or scary, and how to communicate using body language. They find the ⁵(a. lessons interesting b. interesting lessons) and very helpful. Japanese people love cute characters, so finding a job as a mascot is not difficult for graduates of the school.

Notes loose「ゆるい」/ silly「バカげた」/ interact「交流する」/ scary「怖い」/ graduate「卒業生」

B もう一度英文を読み、1～4の英文について適切な語句を選びましょう。

1. *Yuru kyara* make people feel (**a.** relaxed   **b.** young   **c.** silly).
2. Choko is the name of a (**a.** school   **b.** person   **c.** mascot character).
3. Ms. Ohira (**a.** runs a school   **b.** makes mascot costumes   **c.** began wearing mascot costumes in 1985).
4. Students learn (**a.** modern dance   **b.** children's games   **c.** gestures) at the school.

Fun with Words ▶ Gestures

A 1～8のジェスチャーが表す意味をa～hから選びましょう。

1. (　)
2. (　)
3. (　)
4. (　)
5. (　)
6. (　)
7. (　)
8. (　)

a. I did it!   **b.** I don't know.   **c.** I'm not happy.
d. Look at that.   **e.** Please be quiet.   **f.** That's no good.
g. This way, please.   **h.** What did you say?

B 空所に入る適当な表現を **A** から選び、英文を完成させましょう。

1. I'm trying to study. (　　　　　　　　　　　).
2. I'm sorry, I didn't hear you. (　　　　　　　　　　　)?
3. I'll show you to your seat. (　　　　　　　　　　　).

Trees—One of Nature's Wonders

比較

Unit 21

Reading Step 1 — Getting the Picture

A 英文を読んで、話の流れに合うように下の絵を並べましょう。

CheckLink　DL 82　CD2-33

Research shows that living near trees helps people in many ways. For example, people live <u>longer</u> and happier lives when they live in neighborhoods with many trees. Nature makes people feel calm and think positively. Streets with trees are safer than streets without trees, and the crime rate is lower. Trees also help children with short attention spans. These children are able to do an activity longer after a walk in the park. Research also shows that children get better test scores when they live in tree-filled neighborhoods.

Notes neighborhood「近所」/ crime rate「犯罪率」/ attention span「集中力の持続時間」

1 ☐ → 2 ☐ → 3 ☐ → 4 ☐

111

Reading Step 2 Grammar Made Easy

比較級

2つ以上のものを比べて「より…です」と言いたい場合は、比較級を使います。比較級は、形容詞や副詞の語尾に -er をつけて作ります。

| My brother is **younger** than you. | 私の兄はあなたよりも若いです。 |

長めの単語と、語尾が -ly で終わる形容詞、副詞には、前に more をつけて作ります。

| The new computer looks **more expensive** than the old one. | 新しいコンピュータは古いものよりも高価に見えます。 |

比較級の中には、-er や more をつけるだけでは作れないものもあります。

| John can sing **better** than Peter. | ジョンはピーターよりも上手に歌うことができます。 |
| My health condition is **worse** than before. | 私の健康状態は以前よりも悪いです。 |

LOOK BACK もう一度 Reading Step 1 の英文を読んで、比較級に下線を引きましょう。1つ目は2行目の <u>longer</u> です。あと5つ見つけられますか。

A (　) 内の a〜c から適当な語句を選び、○で囲みましょう。

1. Today is (**a.** cold   **b.** colder   **c.** more colder) than yesterday.
2. Fruit is (**a.** healthy   **b.** more healthier   **c.** healthier) than cake.
3. A lion is (**a.** danger   **b.** dangerous   **c.** more dangerous) than a zebra.
4. Akemi's test score was (**a.** worse   **b.** bad   **c.** more worse) than Nao's.
5. I'm taking (**a.** more classes   **b.** more classes than   **c.** more than classes) you.

B 空所に入る適当な語句を下から選び、比較級に変えて、英文を完成させましょう。その後で音声を聞いて答えを確認しましょう。

DL 83   CD2-34

big   careful   new   pretty

1. Allen's car is old. He wants a _____ one.
2. Those flowers are nice, but I think these are _____.
3. Azusa makes many careless mistakes. She needs to be _____.
4. I'd like to have a _____ apartment. This one is very small.

最上級

「最も…です」「いちばん…です」と言いたい場合は、最上級を使います。最上級は、形容詞や副詞の前に the をつけ、語尾に -est をつけて作ります。

| Tom is **the tallest** in his class. | トムはクラスでいちばん背が高いです。 |

副詞の場合は the が省略されることがあります。

| Miki can run **(the) fastest** of the three girls. | ミキは3人の少女の中で最も速く走れます。 |

長めの単語と、語尾が -ly で終わる副詞には、前に the most をつけて作ります。

| This question is **the most difficult** of all. | この質問は全部の中で最も難しいです。 |

最上級の中には、-est や most をつけるだけでは作れないものもあります。

| Ken is **the best** player in the tennis club. | ケンはテニス部の中でいちばん上手な選手です。 |
| This is **the worst** experience of my life. | これは私の人生において最悪の経験です。 |

C ( )内の a〜c から適当な語句を選び、○で囲みましょう。

1. Ron is (a. smartest   b. the smartest   c. the most smart) boy in the class.
2. Fiona is (a. tallest   b. the tallest   c. the tallest of) the three girls.
3. How much is the (a. cheapest   b. most cheap   c. most cheapest) ticket?
4. Max is the (a. most bad   b. worse   c. worst) player on the team.
5. August is (a. the hottest   b. hottest the   c. the most hottest) month of the year.
6. This is the most (a. beauty   b. beautiful   c. beautifully) park in the city.

D 例にならい、( )内の語句を最上級に変えて、英文を完成させましょう。その後で音声を聞いて答えを確認しましょう。

1. He is <u>the richest</u> man in Japan. (rich)
2. The Paris Hotel is _____ hotel in the city. (expensive)
3. This is _____ day of my life! (happy)
4. When is _____ time to visit your country? (good)

Reading Step 3 Getting the Idea

A ( )内のa～bから適当な語句を選び、英文を完成させましょう。その後で音声を聞いて答えを確認しましょう。

Giant sequoias are the world's largest trees. The biggest one is called the General Sherman. It stands 84 meters tall and has a circumference of 31 meters. It weighs 1.2 million kilograms, making it the ¹(**a.** heaviest **b.** tallest) living thing on earth. Giant sequoias can live for 3,000 years or more. The ²(**a.** longest **b.** oldest) one lived more than 3,500 years. Giant sequoias once grew in many parts of the world. Today, they are found only in northern California.

Another giant tree is the redwood. Redwoods have smaller trunks than sequoias, but they are ³(**a.** shorter **b.** taller). The ⁴(**a.** tallest **b.** widest) tree in the world is a redwood named Hyperion. It stands nearly 116 meters. The biggest redwood, called the President, has two billion leaves! Redwoods grow in northern California and southern Oregon and can live to be 2,000 years old.

When logging began in the 1850s, most of the old giant sequoias and redwoods were cut down. They were used to build some of the most ⁵(**a.** beautiful **b.** enjoyable) original buildings in San Francisco, Oakland and Sacramento. Today, most are in protected forests and parks.

Notes giant sequoia「ジャイアント・セコイア」/ circumference「外周」/ redwood「アメリカスギ」/ trunk「幹」/ logging「伐採」/ protected forest「保護林」

B もう一度英文を読み、1〜4の英文について適切な語句を選びましょう。

1. The General Sherman weighs (**a.** 1,200   **b.** 120,000   **c.** 1,200,000) kilograms.
2. Giant sequoias grow in (**a.** many parts of the world   **b.** California and Oregon   **c.** northern California).
3. Hyperion is (**a.** 32   **b.** 84   **c.** 116) meters taller than the General Sherman.
4. Most of the old giant sequoias and redwoods were cut down (**a.** before   **b.** after   **c.** in) 1850.

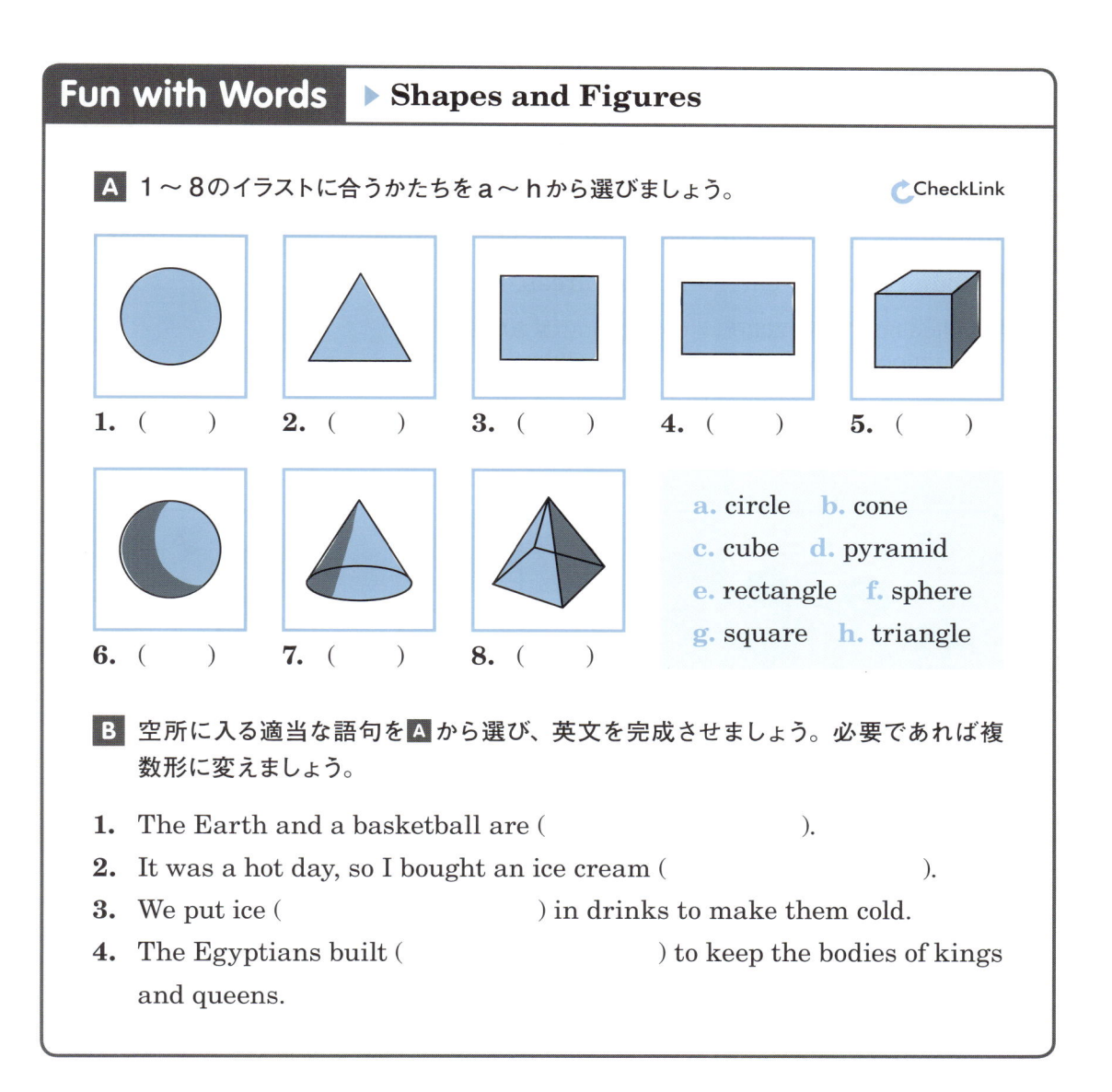

Fun with Words ▶ Shapes and Figures

A 1〜8のイラストに合うかたちをa〜hから選びましょう。

1. (　)   2. (　)   3. (　)   4. (　)   5. (　)

6. (　)   7. (　)   8. (　)

a. circle   **b.** cone
c. cube   **d.** pyramid
e. rectangle   **f.** sphere
g. square   **h.** triangle

B 空所に入る適当な語句を **A** から選び、英文を完成させましょう。必要であれば複数形に変えましょう。

1. The Earth and a basketball are (　　　　　　　).
2. It was a hot day, so I bought an ice cream (　　　　　　　).
3. We put ice (　　　　　　　) in drinks to make them cold.
4. The Egyptians built (　　　　　　　) to keep the bodies of kings and queens.

Unit 22

Koban at Your Service

語句や文をつなぐ接続詞

Reading Step 1　Getting the Picture

A 英文を読んで、話の流れに合うように下の絵を並べましょう。

　　　　　　　　　　　　　　　CheckLink　DL 86　CD2-37

Foreigners living in or visiting Japan are always surprised at how safe the country is. One of the reasons for this is the network of more than 6,000 police boxes, or *koban*. *Koban* are found in towns and cities around the country. Police officers often patrol the area on foot or by bicycle. They talk with local people and respond to emergencies. *Koban* usually have excellent maps, so people often visit them to get directions. Most *koban* are small two-story buildings, but much larger ones can be found in major entertainment areas.

Notes police box「交番、派出所」/ emergency「緊急事態」/
directions「道順」/ two-story「2階建ての」

1 ☐ → 2 ☐ → 3 ☐ → 4 ☐

Reading Step 2 — Grammar Made Easy

語句や文をつなぐ接続詞

2つ以上の語句や文をつなげたい場合は、接続詞を使います。

and 「…と…、…そして…」	I ate <u>ham</u> **and** <u>eggs</u> for breakfast. 私は朝食にハムと卵を食べました。 <u>My father is a pianist</u> **and** <u>my mother is a violinist</u>. 私の父はピアニストで、そして母はバイオリニストです。
or 「…あるいは…、…それとも…」	I want <u>coffee</u> **or** <u>tea</u>. 私はコーヒーあるいは紅茶が欲しいです。 <u>Did you go shopping</u>, **or** <u>did you stay at home</u>? あなたは買い物に行きましたか、それとも家にいましたか。
but 「…しかし…、…ですが…」	<u>I like this hat</u>, **but** <u>it is too big</u>. 私はこの帽子が好きですが、大きすぎます。
so 「…だから…、…なので」	<u>I am hungry</u>, **so** <u>I'll get some hamburgers</u>. 私はお腹がすいているので、ハンバーガーを買います。

LOOK BACK もう一度 Reading Step 1の英文を読んで、語句や文をつなぐ接続詞に下線を引きましょう。1つ目は1行目の <u>or</u> です。あと6つ見つけられますか。

A （　）内のa～dから適当な語句を選び、○で囲みましょう。

1. I had a long day. I'm tired (a. and　b. or　c. but　d. so) hungry.
2. It's raining, (a. and　b. or　c. but　d. so) let's take a taxi home.
3. My car is old, (a. and　b. or　c. but　d. so) it still runs very well.
4. Is Peggy from Australia (a. and　b. or　c. but　d. so) New Zealand?
5. Yohei's father is a doctor (a. and　b. or　c. but　d. so) his mother is a nurse.

B 例にならい、下の接続詞を使って、2つの英文をつなげてみましょう。その後で音声を聞いて答えを確認しましょう。

DL 87　CD2-38

~~and~~　or　but　so

1. Jun went hiking. Kaho went hiking. ⇒ _Jun and Kaho went hiking_.
2. I dropped the glass. It didn't break. ⇒ _____.
3. It's warm. You don't need a coat. ⇒ _____.
4. Would you like coffee? Would you like tea? ⇒ _____?

対応する語句をつなぐ接続詞

「AもBも両方」や「AかBかどちらか」のように、2つの対応する語句をつなげたい場合も、接続詞を使います。このとき、接続詞とよく一緒に使われる語句が、下の3つです。

both A and B 「AとBの両方、AもBも」	**Both** <u>you</u> **and** <u>I</u> like cycling. あなたも私もサイクリングが好きです。
either A or B 「AとBのどちらか、AかBか」	I want to drink **either** <u>water</u> **or** <u>milk</u>. 私は水か牛乳のどちらかを飲みたいです。 I will **either** <u>watch TV</u> **or** <u>read a book</u>. 私はテレビを見るか本を読むかどちらかをします。
neither A nor B 「AとBのどちらも…ない、AでもBでもない」	This movie is **neither** <u>good</u> **nor** <u>bad</u>. この映画はよくも悪くもないです。 I **neither** <u>smoke</u> **nor** <u>drink</u>. 私はたばこも吸わないし、お酒も飲みません。

C （　　）内のa～cから適当な語句を選び、○で囲みましょう。

1. Mike enjoys both playing (a. and　b. or　c. nor) watching sports.
2. I need either your phone number (a. and　b. or　c. nor) your mail address.
3. Peter neither smokes (a. and　b. or　c. nor) drinks.
4. Kana is (a. both　b. either　c. neither) in the cafeteria or in the library.
5. Toru left (a. both　b. either　c. neither) his bag and his umbrella on the train.
6. (a. Both　b. Either　c. Neither) Sota nor Shiho will come to the party.

D 例にならい、(A)と(B)が同じような意味になるよう、空所に入る接続詞を下から選び、英文を完成させましょう。その後で音声を聞いて答えを確認しましょう。　DL 88　CD2-39

　　both … and　　either … or　　neither … nor

1. (A) It is cold today. It is windy today.
   (B) It is <u>both</u> cold <u>and</u> windy today.
2. (A) Tom didn't come. Sally didn't come.
   (B) ＿＿＿＿＿＿＿ Tom ＿＿＿＿＿＿＿ Sally came.
3. (A) We can stay home. We can go dancing.
   (B) We can ＿＿＿＿＿＿＿ stay home ＿＿＿＿＿＿＿ go dancing.
4. (A) He isn't rich. He isn't famous.
   (B) He is ＿＿＿＿＿＿＿ rich ＿＿＿＿＿＿＿ famous.

Reading Step 3 Getting the Idea

A (　)内のa～bから適当な語句を選び、英文を完成させましょう。その後で音声を聞いて答えを確認しましょう。

In 2004, a *koban* was built in London's Piccadilly Circus, the main entertainment district of the city. About 700,000 people pass through Piccadilly Circus every day. The main reasons for building the *koban*, 1(**a.** and **b.** or) "pavilion" as they call it, were to help people with directions and to make visitors to London feel safe. The pavilion is popular with 2(**a.** both **b.** either) Japanese tourists and tourists from other countries. It is open 24 hours a day, 365 days a year.

The pavilion is like the police posts that were common in England in the first half of the last century. The old police posts were very small, 3(**a.** but **b.** so) only one officer worked at each one. They had a telephone that the officer or the public could use. When two-way radios became common in the 1960s, the posts gradually disappeared.

Unlike *koban* in Japan, police officers at the pavilion 4(**a.** either **b.** neither) patrol the area nor investigate crimes. Most visitors to the pavilion either ask for directions 5(**a.** or **b.** nor) report lost items such as mobile phones or wallets.

Notes ▶ district「地区」/ pavilion「仮設の建物、パビリオン」/ as they call it「いわゆる」/ two-way radio「送受信できる無線機」/ investigate「捜査する」/ lost item「落とし物」

B もう一度英文を読み、1〜4の英文について適切な語句を選びましょう。

1. Piccadilly Circus is (**a.** a zoo   **b.** a pavilion   **c.** an area) in London.
2. Police posts were common in England (**a.** between 1900 and 1950   **b.** around 1950   **c.** between 1950 and 2000).
3. Police posts started to disappear in England when (**a.** telephones became common   **b.** two-way radios appeared   **c.** modern police stations were built).
4. Police officers working at the pavilion (**a.** give directions to visitors   **b.** look for criminals   **c.** patrol the area).

Fun with Words ▶ Around Town

A 例にならい、それぞれの英文の続きをa〜hから選びましょう。

1. Go to the fitness center (*g*).
2. Go to a koban (   ).
3. Go to the library (   ).
4. Go to the park (   ).
5. Go to the post office (   ).
6. Go to a restaurant (   ).
7. Go to the supermarket (   ).
8. Go to the zoo (   ).

> **a.** to have a meal   **b.** to ask for directions   **c.** to send a package
> **d.** to take a walk   **e.** to see animals   **f.** to buy some food
> **g.** to do some exercise   **h.** to read a book

B **A**を参考にして、空所に続きを書いてみましょう。

1. Go to a coffee shop (   ).
2. Go to a museum (   ).
3. Go to a bakery (   ).
4. Go to a video shop (   ).

3-D Printers

時や理由などを表す接続詞

Unit 23

Reading Step 1 Getting the Picture

A 英文を読んで、話の流れに合うように下の絵を並べましょう。

3-D printing is nothing new. However, people are only now talking about it <u>because the technology is much better than before, and cheaper</u>. Before 3-D printing begins, a 3-D image of the item is created. This is done using a scanner and a computer-aided design (CAD) software program. After the image is created, it is sliced into thin layers. The layers are then printed, one on top of the other. It takes time to create even one small item since hundreds or thousands of layers require printing.

Notes computer-aided design (CAD)「コンピュータ支援設計」/ thin「薄い」/ layer「層」

1 ☐ → 2 ☐ → 3 ☐ → 4 ☐

Reading Step 2　Grammar Made Easy

時や理由を表す接続詞

「私が駅に着く前に、電車は出発してしまった」や「彼は風邪を引いたので、学校を休んだ」のように、時や理由を表したい場合は、接続詞を使います。

before 「…する前に」	**Before** you eat, you must wash your hands. 食べる前に、あなたは手を洗わなければなりません。
after 「…した後に」	My father started farming **after** he retired. 私の父は退職した後に、農業を始めました。
because 「…なので」	I went to Spain **because** I wanted to watch soccer games. サッカーの試合が見たかったので、私はスペインに行きました。
since 「…なので」	**Since** it's raining, let's stay at home today. 雨が降っているので、今日は家にいよう。

＊becauseとsinceはどちらも理由を表す場合に使いますが、話し手と聞き手の両方がすでに知っている理由を述べるときは、sinceを使います。

LOOK BACK もう一度 Reading Step 1 の英文を読んで、〈時や理由を表す接続詞＋文〉に下線を引きましょう。1つ目は2行目の <u>because the technology is much better than before, and cheaper</u> です。あと3つ見つけられますか。

A （　　）内のa～cから適当な語句を選び、○で囲みましょう。　　*CheckLink*

1. Take off your shoes (a. before　b. after　c. because) you enter the room.
2. (a. Before　b. After　c. Since) we had a big breakfast, let's have a light lunch.
3. Bob always takes a shower (a. before　b. after　c. since) he gets up in the morning.
4. I can't understand Ed's English (a. before　b. after　c. because) he speaks too fast.

B （　　）内の語句を並べ替えて、英文を完成させましょう。その後で音声を聞いて答えを確認しましょう。　　　DL 91　　CD2-42

1. Brush your teeth ＿＿＿＿＿＿＿＿＿＿＿＿＿＿＿＿＿＿＿＿＿＿＿＿＿＿.
(you / go to bed / before)［あなたが寝る前に］
2. I'll call you ＿＿＿＿＿＿＿＿＿＿＿＿＿＿＿＿＿＿＿＿＿＿＿＿＿＿.
(after / in London / arrive / I)［私がロンドンに着いた後に］

時点や期間／条件や譲歩を表す接続詞

「高校生**だったとき**、私はバンドを組んでいました」や「北海道に滞在**していた間**、私はカニをたくさん食べました」のように、ある時点や一定の期間を表したい場合も、接続詞を使います。

when 「…するとき、…したら」	**When** I'm tired, I listen to my favorite music. 私は疲れているとき、お気に入りの音楽を聞きます。
while 「…する間に」	Did you see Jeff **while** you were in New York? あなたはニューヨークにいた間に、ジェフに会いましたか。

「**もし**雨が止んだら、ジョギングに行こう」や「彼女は速く泳げる**けれども**、速く走ることはできない」のように、条件や譲歩を表したい場合も、接続詞を使います。

if 「もし…なら」	**If** you have a question, please email me. もし質問があるなら、私にメールしてください。
unless 「…しないかぎり」	You'll never get anything **unless** you try. 挑戦しないかぎり、あなたは決して何も得られないでしょう。
although/though 「…だけれども」	**Although** I can't run fast, I love running. 私は速く走れないけれども、走ることが大好きです。

C （　）内のa〜cから適当な語句を選び、○で囲みましょう。　　CheckLink

1. (a. Although b. When c. Unless) the weather is fine, I like to walk in the park.
2. Please call me (a. if b. though c. unless) you're going to be late.
3. (a. If b. When c. Though) it is dangerous, many people try to climb Mt. Everest.
4. I fell asleep (a. although b. unless c. while) I was watching the movie.
5. I'm not talking to you (a. if b. unless c. when) you say you're sorry.
6. (a. Although b. When c. If) he's only 25 years old, he has his own company.

D （　）内の語句を並べ替えて、英文を完成させましょう。その後で音声を聞いて答えを確認しましょう。

DL 92　　CD2-43

1. _____, just ask.
   (my help / need / you / if) ［もしあなたが助けを必要とするならば］
2. What were you doing _____?
   (you / the news / when / heard) ［あなたがその知らせを聞いたとき］

123

Reading Step 3 Getting the Idea

A (　　)内のa～bから適当な語句を選び、英文を完成させましょう。その後で音声を聞いて答えを確認しましょう。

CheckLink　DL 93　CD2-44

　Have you ever broken or lost something, and then later learned that it is no longer sold and cannot be fixed? ¹(**a.** Although　**b.** If) 3-D printing technology continues to improve, you may soon be able to print a new one using your own 3-D printer. 3-D printers are amazing machines. They can make almost anything, from plastic toys and metal machine parts to chocolate cakes and human body parts. ◂05

　Printing human body parts may sound like science fiction, but, in fact, it has already been done. ²(**a.** Before　**b.** After) a British man suffered serious head injuries in a motorcycle accident in 2012, doctors rebuilt his face using 3-D printed parts. ³(**a.** Although　**b.** Because) the man was ◂10 wearing a motorcycle helmet at the time of the accident, he broke several bones in his face and suffered a fractured skull. ⁴(**a.** If　**b.** When) the man woke up after the operation, he said the results were "totally life-changing." He looked almost the same as he did ⁵(**a.** before　**b.** after) the accident happened, and he didn't have to wear a hat and glasses to hide ◂15 his injuries.

Notes ▶　no longer ...「もう…でない」/ suffer「(嫌なことを)経験する」/ injury「ケガ」/ fractured「粉々になった」/ skull「頭蓋骨」/ operation「手術」

B もう一度英文を読み、1〜4の英文について適切な語句を選びましょう。

1. The writer thinks that 3-D printers may (**a.** become common household items   **b.** be too expensive for ordinary people to own   **c.** not continue to improve).
2. 3-D printing was used to (**a.** fix the man's motorcycle   **b.** rebuild the man's face   **c.** make a new helmet).
3. After the operation, the man looked like (**a.** he had a plastic face   **b.** someone you might see in a science fiction movie   **c.** he did before the accident).
4. The man wore a hat and glasses (**a.** before his accident   **b.** after his accident   **c.** after his operation).

Fun with Words ▶ For Your Safety

A 1〜8のイラストに合う道具をa〜hから選びましょう。

1. (　　)
2. (　　)
3. (　　)
4. (　　)
5. (　　)
6. (　　)
7. (　　)
8. (　　)

a. gloves   **b.** goggles   **c.** hardhat   **d.** kneepads
e. life vest   **f.** mask   **g.** safety cone   **h.** work boots

B 空所に入る適当な語句を**A**から選び、英文を完成させましょう。

1. Volleyball players wear (　　　　　　　　).
2. Always wear a (　　　　　　　　) when you're on a boat.
3. A brick fell on my foot, but, luckily, I was wearing (　　　　　　　　).

Unit 24 Fashion Trends Start Here

関係詞節

Reading Step 1 — Getting the Picture

A 英文を読んで、話の流れに合うように下の絵を並べましょう。

Fashion trends usually start with fashion designers <u>who design spring and fall collections</u>. Their collections are based on things that have inspired them throughout the season. They then present their collections at fashion shows. When people who have high cultural status such as singers, actors, or sports figures start to wear these new fashions, a fashion trend may start. Similar, but cheaper designs will appear in department stores, shopping malls and boutiques. Some trends that are popular in one country spread to other countries, becoming worldwide sensations.

Notes present「提示する」/ cultural status「文化的地位」/
sports figure「スポーツ選手」/ sensation「興奮、評判」

1 □ → 2 □ → 3 □ → 4 □

Reading Step 2　Grammar Made Easy

関係詞節

「私が買った本」や「私を助けてくれた男性」というように、名詞（「本」「男性」）に説明文（「私が買った」「私を助けてくれた」）をつけ加えたい場合は、関係詞節を使います。関係詞節は前の名詞を説明する働きをして、ほとんどの場合、〈関係代名詞＋説明文〉で成り立っています。

the book [which/that I bought]	本 ＋［私が買った］＝「私が買った本」
名詞＋［関係詞節（関係代名詞＋説明文）］	
the man [who helped me]	男性 ＋［私を助けてくれた］＝「私を助けてくれた男性」
名詞＋［関係詞節（関係代名詞＋説明文）］	

関係代名詞は、関係詞節が説明する名詞を言い換えたもので（上の例では the book ⇒ which/that、the man ⇒ who）、つねに関係詞節の先頭に来ます。また、関係代名詞は、関係詞節の中で、主語（「…は、…が」）、目的語（「…を、…に」）、所有（「（人）の」）の働きをし、どの働きをするかによって形が変わります。関係代名詞は訳す必要はありません。

前の名詞	主格	所有格	目的格
人	who	whose	whom
物	which	whose	which
人／物	that	—	that

LOOK BACK もう一度 Reading Step 1 の英文を読んで、関係詞節に下線を引いてみましょう。1つ目は1行目の who design spring and fall collections です。あと3つ見つけられますか。

A （　）内の a〜c から適当な語句を選び、○で囲みましょう。　CheckLink

1. The movie (a. I saw that　b. that I saw　c. that I saw it) was great.
2. The man (a. he helped　b. who helped　c. who he helped) me was kind.
3. The (a. bus which I take　b. which I take bus　c. bus I which take) is late.
4. Did you see the photos (a. that Ai took　b. that took Ai　c. that Ai took them)?

B （　）内の語句を並べ替えて、英文を完成させましょう。その後で音声を聞いて答えを確認しましょう。

DL 95　CD2-46

1. I love the earrings ＿＿＿＿＿＿＿＿＿＿＿＿＿＿＿＿＿＿＿. (wearing / you're / that)
2. The man ＿＿＿＿＿＿＿＿＿＿＿＿＿＿＿＿＿＿＿ is Jim. (laughing / who / is)
3. Karen is a woman ＿＿＿＿＿＿＿＿＿＿＿＿＿＿＿＿＿＿＿. (can / we / whom / trust)

〈名詞＋関係詞節〉の働き／関係副詞

〈名詞＋関係詞節〉は文の中で主語や目的語、補語になります。

The lady who lives next door is 100 years old. 　　　　　　文の主語	隣に住んでいる女性は100歳です。
I have a friend who is good at playing soccer. 　　　　　　　　文の目的語	私にはサッカーが得意な友だちがいます。
This is the bag that my sister wants to buy. 　　　　　　　文の補語	これが私の姉が買いたがっているバッグです。
The man whose wallet you found is my English teacher. 　　　　　　　　文の主語	あなたが財布を見つけたその男性は、私の英語の先生です。

「私が生まれ育った街」や「あなたと一緒に遊んだ日々」というように、場所や時を表す名詞を説明する関係詞節を作るときは、関係副詞の where や when を使うこともできます。when や where の後には〈主語＋動詞〉が来ます。関係副詞の when や where も訳す必要はありません。

I will never forget the days when we played together. 　　　　　　　　　　文の目的語	私たちが一緒に遊んだ日々を私は決して忘れません。
The house where I grew up is in the next town. 　　　　　　文の主語	私が育った家は隣町にあります。

C （　）内の a〜c から適当な語句を選び、○で囲みましょう。　 **CheckLink**

1. What's the name of the student (a. that　b. who　c. どちらでもよい) came late?
2. The dress (a. that　b. which　c. どちらでもよい) she wore was beautiful.
3. The woman (a. who　b. whose　c. who's) cat you found is very happy.
4. That was the year (a. who　b. when　c. where) I went to England.
5. This is the shop (a. where　b. that　c. when) I bought my computer.
6. Do you know the man (a. who's　b. whose　c. who) standing next to Bill?

D 例にならい、（　）内の関係詞節を正しい位置に入れて、英文を完成させましょう。その後で音声を聞いて答えを確認しましょう。

　DL 96　　CD2-47

1. The box looks heavy. (that he's carrying)
   　　　that he's carrying
2. The town is near the sea. (where I was born)
3. Do you remember the day? (when you proposed to your wife)

Reading Step 3 Getting the Idea

A (　　)内のa～bから適当な語句を選び、英文を完成させましょう。その後で音声を聞いて答えを確認しましょう。

　　If you're looking for street fashion, then Harajuku is the place for you. Every day of the year, thousands of people go there to shop and to look at the newest trends. Harajuku's start as a fashion center came after World War II ¹(**a.** when   **b.** where) the U.S. army barracks were built in what is now Yoyogi Park. They were called Washington Heights. Then shops ²(**a.** that   **b.** whose) served the military families opened. This attracted young Japanese people ³(**a.** where   **b.** who) wanted to learn about Western culture. The Summer Olympic Games came to Tokyo in 1964, and Washington Heights became the Olympic Village, the place ⁴(**a.** when   **b.** where) many of the athletes stayed during the Games. People from all over Japan came to Harajuku, hoping to meet some of the Olympic athletes. Many new shops opened, and Harajuku became Japan's most popular place for fashion.

　　Harajuku is a major tourist spot for foreign visitors to Tokyo, especially Takeshita-dori. Takeshita-dori is a street ⁵(**a.** that   **b.** who) is famous for its many shops targeting young people. Many high school girls with unique and eye-catching fashion tastes can be seen there.

Notes army barracks「(陸軍)兵舎」/ military「軍(人)の」/
athlete「スポーツ選手」/ eye-catching「人目を引く」

B もう一度英文を読み、1〜4の英文について適切な語句を選びましょう。

1. Washington Heights was (**a.** a shopping center   **b.** an army barracks   **c.** a fashion brand).
2. Washington Heights became the Olympic Village (**a.** in 1964   **b.** after the Tokyo Olympics   **c.** during World War II).
3. Japanese people came to the Olympic Village to (**a.** live   **b.** shop   **c.** meet athletes).
4. Harajuku became the most popular fashion spot (**a.** before World War II   **b.** around the time of the Tokyo Olympics   **c.** when foreign visitors started going there).

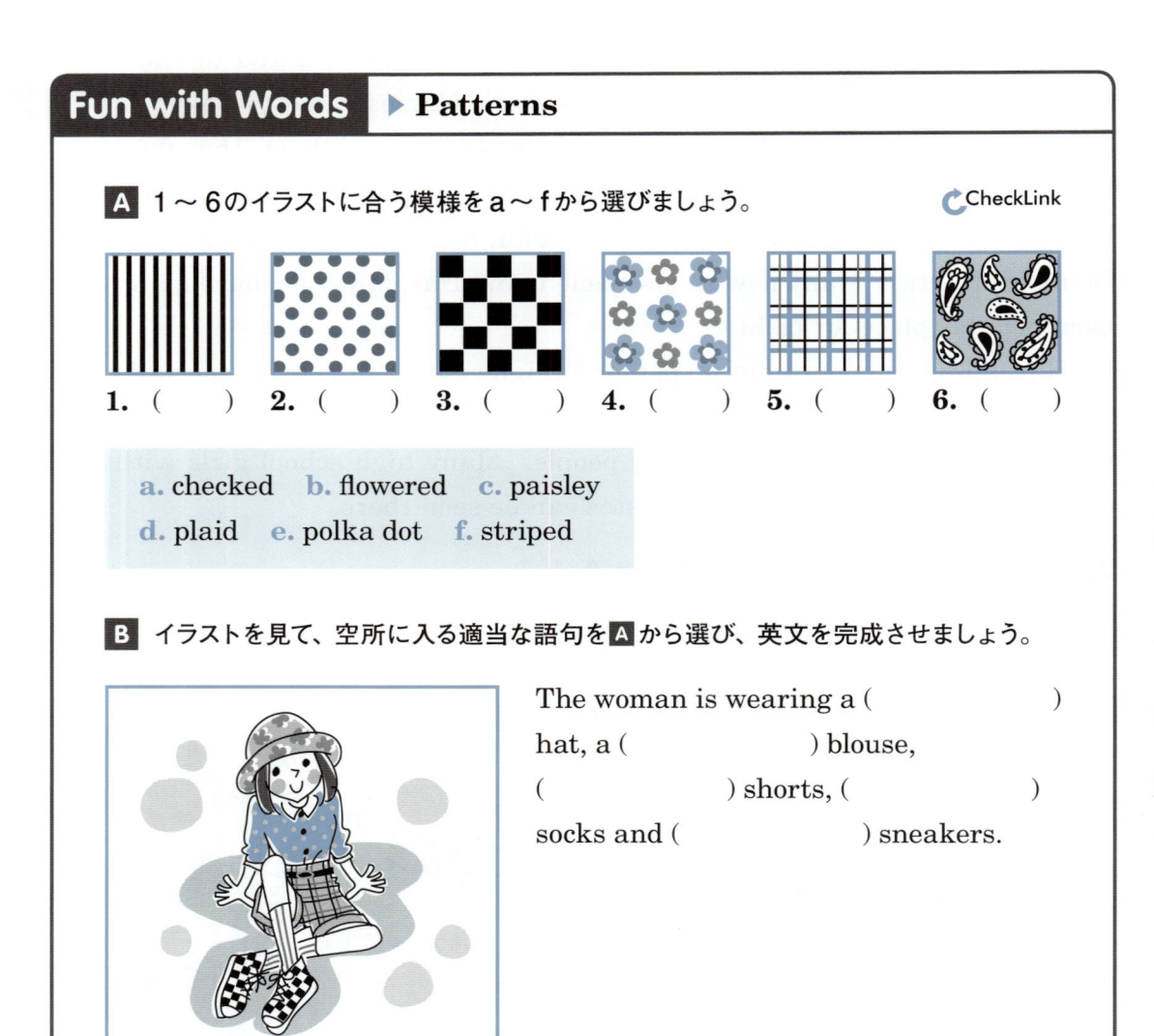

Fun with Words ▶ Patterns

A 1〜6のイラストに合う模様をa〜fから選びましょう。

1. (　)　2. (　)　3. (　)　4. (　)　5. (　)　6. (　)

a. checked   **b.** flowered   **c.** paisley
d. plaid   **e.** polka dot   **f.** striped

B イラストを見て、空所に入る適当な語句を**A**から選び、英文を完成させましょう。

The woman is wearing a (　　　　) hat, a (　　　　) blouse, (　　　　) shorts, (　　　　) socks and (　　　　) sneakers.

本書にはCD（別売）があります

Reading Steps
ステップアップ 英文読解と基本文法

2015年1月20日 初版第1刷発行
2025年2月20日 初版第16刷発行

著 者　Robert Hickling
　　　　臼 倉 美 里

発行者　福 岡 正 人
発行所　株式会社 金 星 堂

（〒101-0051）東京都千代田区神田神保町 3-21
Tel. (03) 3263-3828（営業部）
　　 (03) 3263-3997（編集部）
Fax (03) 3263-0716
https://www.kinsei-do.co.jp

編集担当　今門貴浩　　　　　　　　Printed in Japan
印刷所・製本所／三美印刷株式会社
本書の無断複製・複写は著作権法上での例外を除き禁じられています。本書を代行業者等の第三者に依頼してスキャンやデジタル化することは、たとえ個人や家庭内での利用であっても認められておりません。
落丁・乱丁本はお取り替えいたします。
ISBN978-4-7647-3992-5　C1082